Margaret -

Xmas 1964,

INVEREWE:

A Garden in the North-West Highlands

INVEREWE

A Garden in the North-West Highlands

by

MAY COWAN

1964

GEOFFREY BLES · LONDON

Printed in Great Britain
by The Whitefriars Press Ltd., Tonbridge
and published by
GEOFFREY BLES LTD.

52 DOUGHTY STREET, LONDON, W.C.1
33 YORK STREET, SYDNEY
531 LITTLE COLLINS STREET, MELBOURNE
47–53 CASTLEMAINE STREET, BRISBANE
CML BUILDING, KING WILLIAM STREET, ADELAIDE
WYNDHAM STREET, AUCKLAND
10 DYAS ROAD, DON MILLS, ONTARIO
P.O. BOX 8879, PALLSTATE HOUSE
51 COMMISSIONER STREET, JOHANNESBURG

First published 1964

To the memory of my husband,
who left so much of himself at Inverewe

Preface

The lovely garden of Inverewe will always be a shining tribute to the memory of Osgood Mackenzie, who created it, beginning in 1862; and to his daughter and only child Mrs. Sawyer, who carried on his work when he died in 1922. My husband, John Macqueen Cowan, had intended to contribute to the Centenary celebrations by a book that would bring the story of the garden up to the present day, but his sudden death in 1960 prevented the completion of this task and it then became my privilege to try to do it for him. He had written many notes and had discussed them fully with me, so that what I have written is based very largely on his own work, especially on the subject of Rhododendrons, of which he had a unique knowledge.

I carried on the guardianship of Inverewe during the year 1961, but did not feel able to do it for longer and very reluctantly decided to leave. This difficult decision was made easier for me by the knowledge that whoever took my place would have the loyal support of Kenneth John Urquhart, Mrs. Sawyer's head gardener, who had worked there for 40 years and loved the place as much as Mrs. Sawyer and her father had done and as my husband and I had learnt to love it during our stay there. Unfortunately Murdo Cameron, whose father had worked on the estate before him and had been chosen as the local Bard, had recently retired and his health was failing fast. Murdo Cameron's father was a poet and a stone monument had been erected to his memory near the entrance to Inverewe by Mr. Moffat Pender, a Gaelic scholar himself, even though not Scottish. Our other helpers, too, were close to retiring age, but we were fortunate in having had Donald Gallie with us for most of our stay and we had found him very apt at getting to know the plants and their names and he is now second in command and a great help. William Mackenzie knew the plants very well and could always tell us where they were, even when we had forgotten ourselves; but poor health made him leave soon after me.

Acknowledgements

I wish to express my grateful thanks for much patient help and advice to my publisher, Mr. Jocelyn Gibb, who has known Inverewe for very much longer than I have, and to Mr. George Scott Johnstone, B.Sc., F.R.S.E., District Geologist in charge of the Highland unit of the Geological Survey of Great Britain, for checking what I have written from my husband's notes, and correcting many points. I also owe sincere thanks to our successor at Inverewe, Miss Alice Maconochie, who has kindly noted for me the condition of some of the latest introductions.

Most of the coloured illustrations are taken from my husband's photographs, but I owe a great debt to the Royal Horticultural Society for allowing me to use their blocks, both coloured and black and white, without any charge; and to Mr. Eric Robson, Assistant Secretary (Gardens) to the National Trust for Scotland, for the use of some of his excellent photographs.

Last of all, my very special thanks go to my son and daughter-in-law, Robert and Margaret Cowan, for much help and encouragement, especially in wrestling with the geography of the places from which so many plants have found their way to Inverewe. I am sure that their own interest has been further stimulated to try to grow some more of these plants for themselves and my great hope is that reading this book will have the same effect on many future young gardeners.

Contents

Illustrations

The captions to the plates facing pages 80 and 113 should read:

Plate 13a. MAGNOLIA SIEBOLDII (3)
Platė 13b. MAGNOLIA CAMPBELLII (22)
Plate 18. PELTIPHYLLUM PELTATUM SYN.
SAXIFRAGA PELTATA (19)

5 TO 8 INCLUSIVE ARE IN MONOCHROME

Introduction

This book is in the nature of a sequel to *A Hundred Years in the Highlands*. It might be a fairy story beginning "Once upon a time there was a young man called Osgood Hanbury Mackenzie, who saw a little peninsula of almost barren rock jutting out into the sea, in the midst of the most entrancing scenery, and he decided that here he was going to live and make himself a garden".

Of course he had not just dropped there by chance. His roots were in the soil of the place, because his forebears had been lairds of Gairloch and this was part of their estate, but, being a younger son, he did not inherit it. His mother was the second wife of the previous laird and, when she bought this piece of land for her son, he at once set about the first essential, which was to provide shelter from the fierce gales that he had so often experienced. For this he planted a shelter belt of trees, especially round the seaward side of the peninsula facing the south-west and west, the direction of the prevailing winds. Then, with infinite patience, he waited for 20 years for them to grow, before he began to introduce exotic trees and shrubs, many of which he had seen on his travels, and to site each one with perfect skill. But, before I say any more about the development of the garden, I must give a word of explanation about my husband's and my connection with Inverewe.

Osgood Mackenzie died in 1922 and his daughter, then Mrs. Hanbury, later becoming Mrs. Sawyer, carried on the creation of the garden, as inspired by her father, having done so much of it with him while he was alive. In her later years she feared for the future of this child of his, as she began to realise that she had no close relative who would be able to live at Inverewe and look after it, when she was no longer there. It was then that she approached the National Trust for Scotland. Most fortunately, with the help of endowments (by far the largest being from Mrs. Sawyer herself), they were able to undertake the responsibility of saving this treasure for the enjoyment and inspiration of the people of Scotland and, indeed, of garden lovers the world over. But endowments, though a vital and gratefully accepted necessity, could so easily have been less well handled, if the Trust had not been able to find my husband (who was due to retire in a short time from the Edinburgh Botanic Garden) both free and delighted to be able to share this responsibility with them. His experience in Edinburgh, following his years as an officer in the Indian Forest Service, had given him a deep love for plants and gardening, as well as a sympathetic understanding for people. With these qualities he was able at once to win the respect and affection of the staff.

After Mrs. Sawyer's death we went to live at Inverewe House in June, 1954 and from then onwards it became a matter of ever-increasing urgency for us both to enter into the spirit of Osgood Mackenzie and Mairi Sawyer and to keep the garden essentially theirs, whilst continually adding to the flora and opening up more parts of the woodland, so that larger and larger numbers of visitors could wander unobtrusively through it and savour its strange beauty.

Plate 1. *CYTISUS BATTANDIERI* (25)

[The number shown in brackets after each caption indicates the approximate place of the photograph on the map to be found on pages 144 & 145]

Plate 2a. *MYOSOTIDIUM HORTENSIA* (SYN. *M. NOBILE*) (5 and 6)

Plate 2b. *RHODODENDRON* *COUNTESS OF HADDINGTON* (21)

Plate 2c. *WATSONIA BEATRICIS* (3)

CHAPTER I

Inverewe: Where and What is it?

Situation

The garden of Inverewe is world famous and every year many thousands of visitors find their way there (over 60,000 in 1963), but those who have not yet been so fortunate may like to have a few directions as to how it may be reached. (Please refer also to the map on page 143.)

Inverewe lies about 84 miles due west of Inverness and the train from there to Kyle of Lochalsh may be taken as far as Achnasheen (at any rate at the time of writing). But the remaining 37 miles must be travelled by road and for this there is a 'bus running once a day in each direction, but not so that the return journey from Achnasheen can be accomplished in one day. During the summer months, there are, however, many coaches which carry visitors to Inverewe from Inverness, Dingwall and Strathpeffer and from Ullapool to the North, as well as from much greater distances such as Grantown-on-Spey, Edinburgh, Glasgow, Dundee, Birmingham, Shropshire, Cardiff and even from London, stopping on the way. But the majority of visitors travel by car and would like to know something about the road. From Achnasheen there is but a single track, with frequent passing places, most of which are now large enough to take a coach and several cars; but the road cannot easily be widened enough to make two tracks all the way, because this would involve much blasting of rock and would spoil the scenery, as well as making it possible for cars to travel far too fast to enjoy it. The surface of the road has been greatly improved in recent years and is now very good.

When travelling by road two approaches are possible. The road from Inverness forks left about a mile after passing Garve and at this point we may follow the railway line to the left; or we may take the Ullapool road to the right and, after covering 29 miles on this road, we reach Braemore junction and here we take the fork to the left and very soon see one of the best of the Highland waterfalls, The Falls of Measach, in Corrieshalloch Gorge, which is the property of the National Trust for Scotland. The best view of these falls can, however, be had by continuing along the Ullapool road for about one mile beyond the junction and then, where there is a notice, going down a short steep path to the edge of the gorge, where a small platform has been built, jutting out from the bank, and from here an excellent view of these spectacular falls can be had. Then we must return to the Braemore junction and take the road to Dundonnell, rising to a height of 1000 ft. over a long stretch of uncultivated moorland, which is liable to be blocked by snow in winter. Now and again deer may be seen browsing and in the background are the hills of the An Teallach range with their curious rugged peaks and steep ridges of white quarzite slabs. The descent, through Strath Beg, is by the side of the Dundonnell river to the head of Little Loch Broom. From Dundonnell Hotel the road follows the loch and then rises to the head of the watershed and drops again to the beautiful sands of Gruinard Bay, with the view across it to the Summer Isles and beyond them some of the world's oldest mountains, Stac Polly, Suilven and Ben More Coigach. Then comes a steep ascent and one feels on top of the world and can look back to Scourie and the islands of Sutherland in the north, to the island of Lewis in the west, with nothing but sea between it and Labrador, and southwards as far as Applecross.

Then there is a winding course past two small townships known as Second Coast and First Coast and on to Laide and Aultbea; and from the high ground above Aultbea the whole prospect of Loch Ewe opens before the traveller, with the small Isle Ewe near at hand and Lewis again in the distance. Nearer Tournaig the hills of Beinn Aridh Charr and the magnificent prospect of the whole Torridon range come into view and soon Inverewe is reached.

If, after passing Garve, we had taken the left fork in the road we would pass Loch Luichart and two large power stations, before reaching Achnasheen, not inappropriately named as "the field of storms". Beyond Achnasheen the road to Inverewe leaves the railway and forks to the right, then, after skirting Loch Rosque, climbs for about three miles to the top of the watershed, 804 ft. above sea level, and descends through Glen Dochartie, a typical Highland glen, to Kinlochewe. On a clear day the view from a little below the summit is superb, especially in August and September when the heather is in flower, with the whole length of Loch Maree (16 miles) extending into the far distance. In winter this road through the glen is occasionally blocked by snow and one wild winter night we spent three hours near the summit, awaiting the clearance of two snow ploughs which had been stuck in drifts, one being completely broken down.

As we approach Kinlochewe, the peaks of the Torridon range come into view, Ben Eighe (the jagged file-like mountain), the highest mountain in the parish of Gairloch and now a Nature Reserve, being the most prominent. The name Kinlochewe signifies in gaelic "the head of Loch Ewe" as it would have been at the time when Loch Maree, instead of being a fresh water loch, was connected with Loch Ewe and formed a branch of the sea which extended inland some 18 miles further than it does at present. This was before the intermediate land was elevated and cut off Loch Maree from the sea.

The road branch for Torridon is passed on the left and at the head of Loch Maree, some two miles further on, is the Giant's Point from which a steamer used to run to the other end of the loch. On the other side of the loch is a high waterfall which is spectacular after a heavy downpour, though marked by little more than a thin black line in a period of drought. The road now runs along the shore of the loch, through a forest of gnarled trees of Scots Pine of the Caledonian type to which Osgood Mackenzie refers in his book, to Grudidh bridge, with Ruadh Stac (the red steep rock) in the distance to the left. From Grudidh to Talladale the road is open, commanding magnificent views across the loch, dominated by the heights of Slioch on the further side. From its summit (3217 ft. high) the channelled slopes sweep down abruptly to the waterside.

Loch Maree Hotel, famous for its fishing, was built in 1872 and was visited by Her Majesty Queen Victoria from 12th to 18th September 1877, commemorated by a Gaelic inscription on a slab of Torridon red sandstone. Near by a stone is pointed out on which Her Majesty sat and sketched and I remember a 'bus driver pointing out to the company that it had to be a large one because she was "broad in the bream"!

After passing through the forest of Slatadale and continuing for some distance the road descends by the Kerry Falls power station and continues alongside the Kerry river and another mile through woodland to Charlestown and the beginning of the village of Gairloch. About 400 yds to the right is Flowerdale House, the site of the older Tighe Dige, associated for many generations with the old Mackenzie chiefs of Gairloch and still occupied for short periods by the present laird.

To the left is the harbour and opposite the Church of

Scotland is a large hollow in the sandy turf-covered soil (now part of the golf course) known as Leabaidh na Ba Baine (the bed of the white cow) which is remembered as a meeting place where communion services were held. A long account of one of these meetings written by Dr. Mackenzie is recorded by Dixon in his book on Gairloch. "It was naturally formed beyond memory of man and, as we knew well, by Fingal for a bed where his white cow was to calve. It had a complete coat of beautiful inch-long benty grass, and a thousand spades could not have formed a more perfectly egg-shaped cup, in the bottom of which was placed the wooden preaching box and in front of it long narrow tables and benches for the communion. A few "shuparior pershons" sent before them stools etc. on which to sit, see and listen, but 99 of the 100 of us sat on the nicely sloping banks all around the "bed" till they overflowed on to the level of the equally grassed ground outside. The "bed" was estimated to hold 2000 persons seated, and perhaps 3000 were often gathered in all to the services, packed tight to one another, as was the popular fashion at these times. . . . I should be very much surprised if anyone who once heard an old Gaelic psalm floating in the air, from the thousands of worshippers in the "bed" could forget it in a 100 years."

From the top of the hill are fine views of the sandy beaches of Gairloch, with the village of Strath beyond and, over an expanse of sea, with nearer mountains and islands, to the hills of Skye on the far side of the minch. Osgood Mackenzie is buried in the churchyard near here.

Beyond Achtercairn the road mounts again with views of the Cuchullins when the day is clear. Below, in a grove of trees, is the Established Church manse, in the building of which Hugh Miller, the author and geologist, took part, as a mason's lad, in about 1823. The road skirts

Loch Tollie for over a mile and, upon the small island near its shore, there was once a fortress occupied by the MacBeaths and later by the McLeods. It is recorded that in the fifteenth century two brothers of Allan McLeod, the laird of Gairloch who was living in this fortress, came over from Lewis, murdered their brother, kidnapped his two sons and carried them off to the far end of the loch, where they were put to death: because Allan had married a Mackenzie and they were determined that their family should have no Mackenzie blood in their veins.

From the junction of the road to Tollie farm there is a fine view of Loch Maree with the slope of Beinn Aridh Charr rising above it. Halfway up Loch Maree is the forest-clad Isle Maree, connected with St. Maelrubha, who brought christianity from Ireland to this part of Scotland in the seventh century, and having a celebrated well, whose waters are said to have magical powers, and a tree into which nails and hundreds of pennies have been driven by patients who came to sample its magic. On a good day the road up Glen Dochartie is visible at a distance of 15 or 16 miles from this viewpoint.

On descending Croft Brae a glimpse of Inverewe is to be had in the distance and, after following the River Ewe and crossing it in the village of Poolewe, we are only half a mile from Inverewe.

As well as the approach to Inverewe by roads from the north and the south there is an even pleasanter one by sea. Loch Ewe was used as a convoy-collecting station during the last two wars and is well known to many sailors who have entered it and climbed steep rocky butments to land eventually at Aultbea. Thirty years ago steamers ran regularly from Oban, taking a day, and it is said that many tourists came by this route. Now you can come either in your own launch or in one belonging to the "Meteor" which will put you ashore comfortably in the garden. She is chartered annually by the National Trust for

Scotland for cruises to Gardens, Islands or Castles and these cruises are exceedingly popular.

Climate

One of the strange peculiarities of the Western Highlands is the aptitude of its climate for sudden and unexpected change and nowhere is this more marked than at Inverewe. With little warning a cloudless sky may turn to a driving mist or rain which obscures all views; or a wild and raging gale in the evening, tossing the sea into great white-crested waves and rocking the roots of the tallest trees, will be followed by a morning of perfect calm. Or again, days will be summer-like in winter and many flowers, such as the Kaffir Lily, in bloom for Christmas and on to the end of the year, only to be blasted by severe frost in a night. Or we may have wintry days in July, with gales smashing many of the best flowers in the Herbaceous Border, or a late frost turning a wealth of Rhododendron flowers to a dingy brown.

The strange thing, too, is that these conditions in the north-west are often just the reverse of what is happening further south. One winter, when the Riviera was deep in snow and even friends of ours who had gone to Naples for a really warm holiday were shivering with frost and snow, Inverewe was enjoying a Riviera-like climate of warmth and sunshine.

The rainfall, too, is equally unpredictable and contrary as well. For example in 1959, while the rest of the country was enjoying, in July and August, the driest and warmest weather experienced for many years, at Inverewe it was unusually and unpleasantly wet; whereas in the previous year we, at Inverewe, enjoyed more than our share of warmth and sunshine, with very little rain throughout the holiday season and elsewhere it was reputed to have been about the wettest in living memory.

This sharp contrast in weather conditions is evident

enough in the comparative rainfall figures for 1958 and 1959, but their study reveals nothing of the sudden changes that occur or the severe gales that accompany dry periods as well as wet ones. The rainfall during 1959 was 69·48 in., whereas in 1958 it had been 51·70 in., the average for the years that records have been kept being 60 in. Of course much depends on how this rainfall is spread through the months. Periods of drought are not unusual in April or May or October, or perhaps at other times instead, or the rain may fall consistently, with short breaks only, throughout the whole season.

One year March was a month almost without rain—from 2nd March to 2nd April only a trace—occasionally mild and sunny, but more often with a cold and biting, drying wind making planting in the garden impossible. March is the month for heather burning on the hills, so that grass can grow for grazing, and that year the drought made the burning all too easy. One night, when we happened to look out at about midnight, we saw that a fire on the other side of the loch had become completely out of control and set the whole hillside ablaze. The result was spectacular, flames leaping high into the sky, clouds of white smoke rolling over the hill tops, with the moon shining above and the whole scene multiplied by the brilliant reflections in the calm waters of Loch Ewe, making a realistic picture of a violent inferno.

Inverewe is not often troubled with heavy falls of snow, but in January, 1959, it fell to a depth of 10 in. in the garden and lay for six weeks, a most unusual occurrence there. Most winters there is a little snow from time to time and the surrounding hill tops are usually covered, so that the view from the windows is reminiscent of holidays in Switzerland. The clear white of the nearby hills often reminded us of the years we spent at Kalimpong on the Himalayas, when we looked out from the forest bungalow on the full glory of the far distant Kanchenjunga range.

The climate, as far as temperature goes, is a fairly equable one, with only a few very exceptional days. On July 2nd, 1958, a temperature of 85° F. was recorded and 21° F. on 6th February of that year.

Shelter

The importance of shelter in an exposed West Coast garden such as Inverewe cannot be over-emphasised. The ideal form of shelter is, of course, a woodland with an undergrowth of wind-resisting shrubs or a woodland supplemented with shrubs planted as informal hedges. Protection is required, not only against wind, but also against salt spray.

Osgood Mackenzie in *A Hundred Years* describes the difficulties he had in establishing shelter. He found *Pinus sylvestris*, the ordinary "shop" Scots Pine, to be "A dreadfully delicate tree when exposed to Atlantic gales", but he obtained about 100 sturdy plants of the Caledonian type from Loch Maree-side and these and the Austrian Pine he describes as (seen from his drawing room window) "some bright green specks appearing above the heather" after an interval of four or five years. He recommends, were he beginning again, to plant first a row of *Pinus montana* (a synonym of *Pinus mugo*) just above the high water mark, then behind it a row of *Pinus austriaca* (a synonym of *Pinus nigra*, the Austrian Pine), followed by a third row of *Pinus laricio* (which is in fact another form of *Pinus nigra*). He evidently intended for this third row var. *calabrica*, the Corsican Pine, as he remarks that "for rapidity of growth on bad soil and on exposed sites no species can compare with the Corsican Pine" and further that it is "proof against cattle, sheep, deer and rabbits, as is no other tree that I know of". He obviously did not then know of the value of Sitka Spruce which is probably as proof against rabbit and sea spray as any of those he mentioned. It is, however, particularly vulnerable to drought, as we found later. Behind this triple outer protective belt, he continues "I would start putting in my ordinary forest trees—Scots pine, silver firs, sycamores, oaks, beeches etc." After some 15–20 years, when some shelter had been established, he "began cutting out some of the commoner stuff, especially my enemies, the "shop" Scots firs, as I call them, which continue to get blasted by the gales of the ocean. Then it was I began planting all sorts of things in the cleared spaces—Douglas Firs, *Abies Albertiana*, copper beeches, sweet and horse chestnuts, *Abies nobilis*, *A. Pinsapo*, *A. lasiocarpa*, *A. Nordmanniana*, *Cupressus macrocarpa*, *C. Lawsoniana*, *Thuja gigantea*, bird cherries, scarlet oaks etc. and now these trees appear almost as if they had formed parts of the original plantation." He mentions, also, planting some varieties of Eucalyptus.

Looking at the woodland today, nearly 100 years after the original planting, these remarks are of great interest. It appears that the whole of the peninsula, with the exception of the open ground in front of the Lodge, along the avenue, the vegetable garden and in front of Inverewe House, was eventually planted and this, with the earliest planting, was, no doubt, undertaken soon after the property was acquired in 1862, as Osgood Mackenzie records; but it seems likely that this was confined to a smaller area. Judging by a count of the annual rings on trees that have fallen, the greater part seems to have been planted about 1880 and this fits in with the building of the old house, which was completed in 1879.

Another point of considerable interest is the fact that the vastly predominating species in the woodland is, strangely enough, Scots pine, so that the "shop" variety cannot have been as much of a failure as we are led to suppose. In the most exposed places growth has certainly been poor, a good many trees are not more than 15–20 ft. high and many have died, but, where there has been some shelter and some soil, trees of excellent commercial quality have been grown and, from a timber merchant's point of view, are now mature.

All the other species mentioned are to be found, though only sporadically, but, in addition to these, there are a good number of larch, some above the Lodge (about 30 years old) of recent planting. We only found a single tree of *Thuja gigantea*, a stump, with coppice shoots, of *Castanea sativa*, no well known horse chestnut and no scarlet oaks. The largest *Cupressus macrocarpa*, 68 ft. high, was blown down by a storm six years ago. Beech, however, has done exceedingly well and there is a grove of sycamore and alder which has stood up to every gale; but, as well as small clearings made for special plantings, areas of a considerable extent have, from time to time, been devastated by gales since the wood was first established. The largest of these windfalls occurred on 17th January, 1953, when a north east gale felled every tree on a strip across the peninsula, extending to some five acres. Near the viewpoint and below the shelter hut similar devastations, on a lesser scale, occurred in earlier years and a gale from the north-east is apt to do much more damage than one from the prevailing south-west. Scarcely a year passes without a number of trees being blown down, 145 in one winter six or seven years ago, but usually much smaller numbers and, considering the lack of soil to anchor them, it is, perhaps, astonishing that there have not been more. The only victim of a recent storm was a single very large beech with its roots flattened and spread out on a rock only a foot below the surface.

When we came to Inverewe we devoted much thought to the problem of maintaining adequate shelter where most of the trees were matured. We considered the felling and re-planting of a protective strip, well within an outside marginal protective belt, but there would be considerable risk in the making of such openings and, with the advice of various Forest Officers, we decided against it. As well as "mature" trees, which may still have a very long life-time ahead of them, there are throughout the policies trees at every stage of their development and, even if gales reduce this sheltering cover still further, as probably they will, it is unlikely that a very large area will be blown at one time. Damage is more likely to occur in sections and it should be possible to maintain enough shelter by regarding the forest as a selective one, leaving the removal of trees to storms, rather than artificial felling, and depending upon natural regeneration and some artificial planting to fill up gaps as they occur. This is the method that we adopted during my husband's last five years at Inverewe and, wherever we found gaps on exposed situations, they were re-planted. The species used included the Austrian Pine, the Mountain Pine and the Scots Pine, as well as the Japanese Larch (*Larix leptolepis*), the Sitka Spruce (*Picea sitchensis*), the Western Hemlock (*Tsuga heterophylla*) and the Common Beech (*Fagus sylvatica*), with underplanting where the canopy was only partially open. Some hundreds of each of these species were used (though most of the Sitka Spruce was soon killed by drought), but purposely we made no attempt to fill in blanks where sufficient surrounding shelter could be provided and, in this way, we left space for further development of the garden.

Well established belts of Rhododendron hybrids, such as *R.* Cynthia and *R.* × *fastuosum flore pleno*, and of species of the Triflorum Series, particularly *R. ambiguum*, provide a considerable amount of shelter. At some early date in the history of the garden, hedges of *R. ponticum* were planted near parts of the periphery. Mrs. Sawyer, writing in the Illustrated Guide, regards this as one of the mistakes made at Inverewe because she and one of her friends in particular hated the sight of "that horror" and says that she would plant instead *Griselinia littoralis* and *Escallonia* × *langleyensis*; but we disagreed with this, because, on a peaty soil where it does grow freely, there is no better shelter than is afforded by *R. ponticum*. It is true that thousands of seedlings must be grubbed up, but, if they are not more than three to four years old, this is not a serious matter and the best sheltered part of the garden depends for its shelter upon a wide belt of *R. ponticum* which is not occupying useful space to the exclusion of more desirable planting. Moreover, where considerable length of shelter is required, plants of *R. ponticum* may be readily obtained whereas *G. littoralis* would be difficult to find in sufficient numbers; and, in addition, *R. ponticum* can make a neat and well-trimmed hedge without involving great labour, as is seen along the avenue, outside the Lodge and near the Mansion House. It requires cutting only once a year (about the third week of July) and is magnificently draped with the Chilean Flame Creeper, *Tropaeolum speciosum*, making a blaze of scarlet blossoms followed by blue berries, in August and September. There is only one place at Inverewe where *R. ponticum* has been allowed to get out of hand and that is where it occurs as undergrowth in a young larch plantation above the Lodge and there it could be brought in hand without great difficulty, should this area be required for future development.

Griselinia littoralis is, none the less, excellent as shelter, particularly for enclosing plots for special planting and, since it seeds and regenerates freely at Inverewe, it is not difficult to obtain a fair number of seedlings if these are required and we raised a large number of plants from cuttings in our propagating frames. Other plants which have proved useful for shelter belts or hedges are *Escallonia macrantha*, *E.* × *langleyensis*, *Olearia macrodonta*, *Arundinaria nitida* and *Phormium tenax*.

Over and above these a considerable number of wind-hardy plants can be selected for planting in exposed places; but shelter of one kind or another must be regarded as Inverewe's greatest need.

Geology and Soil

The head of the peninsula on which Inverewe House stands is known in Gaelic as Am Ploc Ard, The High Lump, because it consists of a high protruding promontory of red sandstone rock. The view from this point or from the House, looking across the loch to the cliffs behind the village or to the steep rocky Craig Tollie, is of rocks of a totally different character. They are of Archaean Gneiss (Lewisian Gneiss) and, according to geological record, are among the oldest rocks known in any part of Britain—or indeed, any part of the world. The sharp contrast between these rocks on either side of the loch is explained by the great geological Fault, which follows the line of Loch Maree, from the Docherty, along the loch, and down the River Ewe to Inverasdale, and by which the rocks on the southern side have been considerably displaced. In their normal sequence the rocks on the south side, of Lewisian Gneiss, are overlaid by the Torridonian Sandstone, which forms the rock on the north or garden side. By the intervention of the Loch Maree Fault, however, both rocks appear, in this view, to be at about the same level.

Both these types of rock are widespread in this part of the North-West Highlands and the actual junction between the two formations can be examined at various places not far from Inverewe, for example, on the shore beneath the Free Church Manse at Gairloch, or in a cutting near Sheildaig, and on Slioch, where the summit is of Torridonian sandstone and overlies the Lewisian Gneiss below. Denudation, by the removal of much of the original rock, has very much affected the aspect of the countryside as a whole. Loch Maree, as geologists can show, was once a great glacier which spread out into the sea by numerous arms, its wanderings evidenced by various markings on the sandstone rock here and there and by the debris of moraines which may be observed between Aultbea and Laide. The site which the garden occupies was, at one time, covered by this great glacier. The Torridonian Sandstone, which outcrops, as cliffs and as boulders, at many places in the garden, is never far below the surface. It is of a reddish chocolate colour and makes a sharp colour contrast with the greens of the foliage which surrounds it. To uncover the rock, all that is necessary, often, is to remove a foot or two of turf.

This Torridonian sandstone is a rock of moderate hardness, not difficult to blast, as has had to be done for the making of roads and paths, and in places it tends to break down into rather small pieces, leaving niches where plants can be established. It disintegrates into a stony, gravelly, unfertile soil, exposed on banks and, here and there, where overlying peat has been removed. The surface soil of the greater part of the garden is pure peat, exceedingly acid (*pH* 3.5), excellent for growing ericacious plants, Primulas, Meconopsis and the like, provided it is broken up and well drained, but apt to dry out completely during periods of prolonged drought. Trees grow well when they are established, but their roots are usually very near the surface because of the closely underlying rock. Rhododendrons are particularly suitable for this shallow soil, because their roots naturally form a dense mat near the stem. This allows them to be easily moved, even when large.

When planting new plants into this pure peat, there is often a check, until they become adjusted to the environment, and this check, with Rhododendrons, usually lasts for a period of two to three years. It may be more or less severe with other genera—Sorbus and Birch come away rapidly, but various conifers and other trees, such as Magnolia and Embothrium, take longer to become established, even when the peat has been well broken and they have been planted with care, The reason for the check is, no doubt, that, as the result of a high permanent water level, air is excluded from the soil, so that tree roots are confined to the surface, where available food is lacking, and are exposed to extremes of moisture and of temperature. If growth proceeds, the roots press further downwards and, in time, sufficiently aerate the lower soil for growth to become normal.

We found that, when planting beds of herbaceous plants, it was often an advantage to mix in soil and sand. One of the difficulties is, indeed, to obtain soil and this lack persisted until the Restaurant and Car Park were made, when the surface of the field had to be removed and this soil was carefully preserved. Earth for the vegetable garden, when it was originally made, had all to be imported.

Plate 3a. DAFFODILS NEAR THE LODGE (1 & 2)

Plate 3b. INVEREWE AND THE BARD'S CAIRN (25)

Plate 4a. THE HOUSE AND HERBACEOUS BORDER FROM THE EAST (4)

Plate 4b. *RHODODENDRON CAMPYLOCARPUM* (17)

CHAPTER II

Creators of the Garden

As I have already mentioned, Mr. Osgood Hanbury Mackenzie became proprietor of Inverewe in 1862. The estate to which the name "Inverewe" was given came into being by the purchase of three properties—of Kernsary, with the exception of the strip extending from Inveran to Londubh, which was retained by the Trustees of Gairloch estate to preserve the fishing rights on both sides of the River Ewe—of Lochend or Kinloch which included the land on which Inverewe House now stands—and of Tournaig, both of which were bought from Sir William Mackenzie of Coul. Inverewe estate at that time extended to some 12,800 acres, stretching to the slopes of Beinn Aridh Charr (the mountain of the rough shieling) and to Fionn (white) Loch, famous then and now for its fishing. Tournaig was sold in 1945 and part of Kernsary in 1952, leaving the garden without the policie, Strondubh farm with 30 acres of arable land and 2000 acres of moorland and rough grazing, with three small lochs and access to two others.

In *A Hundred Years in the Highlands* Osgood Mackenzie records that he was born "on the 13th of May, 1842, at the Chateau de Talhouet, not far from the little town of Quimperlo, in the Morbihan, Brittany". His father was Sir Francis Mackenzie, fifth baronet and twelfth laird of Gairloch, his mother (Sir Francis' second wife) Mary Hanbury. Osgood had two half-brothers, Kenneth (who became sixth baronet and thirteenth laird of Gairloch, 10 years older than himself, and Francis one year younger than Kenneth. They returned to England when Osgood was one year old and, while they were still in the south, his father became ill and died suddenly. His body was then taken by sea from London to Invergordon to be buried in the family burial ground in the Old Priory of Beauly. In his will Osgood's father had appointed his mother and Thomas Mackenzie, the laird of Ord, to be trustees for the Gairloch property during his elder half-brother's minority and his uncle, John Mackenzie M.D., to be factor.

For the first year or so after his father's death the mother and son resided at Conon House, the east coast residence of the family; but then she thought it her duty to move to Gairloch, where there was a large crofter population, and make that her permanent home. Travelling in those days was not easy, but by then a road had been made from Dingwall as far as Kinlochewe and, indeed, two miles further to Rudha n'Thamhair (the Giant's point) at the upper end of Loch Maree. Beyond this point there was no road and, to reach Gairloch, it was necessary to travel by rowing boat, an uncomfortable journey in roughish weather.

So Osgood Mackenzie came to live at Gairloch when he was about two years old, and Tigh Dige or Flowerdale, as English tourists suggested it might be called, because of the richness of the wild flora in a nearby glen, was to be his home. He tells us how at a very early age he became interested in plants and birds and other animals, how he learnt to shoot and to swim and fish, both in the sea and in the freshwater lochs and how, when somewhat older, he accompanied his mother on a Shetland pony, as she rode about on horseback, attending to the welfare of the community and to business connected with the estate. "Few men" he remarked later "have done more shooting in their time than I have".

Dixon relates that one of the concerns of the Dowager

Lady of Gairloch was the re-organising of the runrig system of cultivation under which five or six small tenants living together in adjacent houses cultivated the "rigs", into which their arable land was divided, in rotation which was sometimes decided by lot. Instead of this system she introduced crofts of about four acres, each with its own house upon it which was healthier for the population. Osgood records that she further improved their lot by starting some nine or ten new schools, and another work on which she was engaged was the arranging for the distribution of measures of relief during the years of famine caused by the potato blight disease between the years of 1846 and 1848. She herself wrote "When the government steamers called in at Gairloch enquiring as to the distress and poverty caused by the potato disease I did not advocate the sending of supplies of meal etc., but urged continually in speaking and by letters to the Destitution Committee (Edinburgh) and to the Home Secretary that money might be granted to make a road from Rudha n'Thamhair to Slattadale and thus to open the country". Eventually money was granted and the first sod of the new road was cut, in the absence of his eldest brother (as he tells us) by Osgood Mackenzie. Neighbouring proprietors, too, obtained grants and, at about the same time, roads were also built from Kerrysdale to Red Point; from Strath to Melvaig; through the Kerry Glen to Poolewe and on to Cove; and from Poolewe to Aultbea and thence to Dundonnell and join the Ullapool road at Braemore.

When the trusteeship ended in 1853, Sir Kenneth having reached his majority, Lady Mackenzie and Osgood went abroad for a couple of years, mostly in Germany and Switzerland. Osgood had never been to school, but from the age of 11, he had a French tutor and others from time to time. On their return from this journey and before other visits abroad they lived for a time at Pool House and also at Inveran near Poolewe and Osgood took the opportunity of obtaining the shooting rights over part of the property that was later to be his.

He tells us that at about the age of 19 "we were not very expert in flowers" but he had it in mind to propose to purchase the Inverewe property when he paid a visit to Kerrysdale farm to discuss the matter with his granduncle Captain Kenneth Mackenzie, who had lived there for over 70 years and had brought up a large family there, being then over 90 years of age. He was keen on flowers and trees and, in talking of his garden, Osgood remarks that he will always remember the smell of Daphne and Ribes there and the big clumps of *Gladiolus cardinalis*, which was not common in those days, and the line of Christmas Roses which flourished and bloomed in winter and early spring. On hearing of the prospect the old gentleman brightened up and announced "If you, Osgood, make a garden there, I guarantee you will grow good raspberries in it".

And so it came about that in the following year a decision was made to purchase the new estate for him and this his mother did. At that time there were no trees upon the ground which was as bare as the rest of the ground in the vicinity, covered only with grass and heather and crowberry, except for a single dwarf willow, about 3 ft. high, which was preserved for a long time as a curiosity.

When it had been decided where the house would be built—on the neck of the peninsula—Osgood "perfectly ignorant of everything connected with forestry and gardening", as he said, began to build a fence to keep sheep off the ground, while his mother "undertook the whole trouble of house-building".

The construction of the avenue and the making of the walled garden, with its high retaining wall (in places as much as 36 ft. high) was a work which occupied three or

Plate 5a. THE PENINSULA AND THE FIRST HOUSE: 1900

Plate 5b. FROM THE AIR: *Circa* 1920

Plate 6a. *RHODODENDRON SINOGRANDE* (17 and 20)

Plate 6b. A TREE FERN, *DICKSONIA ANTARCTICA* (6)

four years. "The soil of this old sea beach was a 4 ft. mixture of about three parts pebbles and one part of rather nice blackish earth." The old Kinloch house, a one-storied building, thatched with heather, had been situated here. "The millions of pebbles had to be got rid of. So, in deep trenching it, digging forks were mostly used, every workman had a girl or boy opposite him, and the process of hand picking much resembled the gathering of a very heavy crop of potatoes in a field. The cost of the work was great, as thousands upon thousands of barrow-loads of small stones had to be wheeled into the sea and the place of the pebbles made up with endless cartloads of peaty stuff from old turf dykes, red soil carted from long distances and a kind of blue clay marl from below the sea, full of decayed oyster shells and crabs and other good things hauled up at very low tides. There is also a terrace the whole length of the garden cut out of the face of a steep brae which was just above the old beach. It had to be carved out of the solid gravel and covered with soil brought from afar."

While all this was going on, the work of planting the promontory with forest trees was begun, in order to provide shelter from the devastating winds that swept across it. Their growth was very slow at first and Osgood relates that "For four or five years my poor peninsula looked miserable, but at last we could see some bright green specks appearing above the heather. These were the Austrians and the few home-bred Scots Firs which had been dotted about in places of honour near the house. About the fifth or sixth year everything began to shoot ahead; even the little hardwood trees".

Forestry operations took precedence over gardening in the earlier years. Yet there is clear evidence that gardening was by no means entirely neglected. Within the walled garden and probably along the avenue, where the Rhododendrons made a wonderful show in later years, as well as in the immediate precincts of the house, there must have been some ornamental planting. What had been done was enough to have impressed Dixon when he published his book in 1886 and also to have elicited praise from a correspondent to *The Times* who had visited Poolewe in 1883 and is quoted by Dixon, This is what was said "From the village of Poolewe the house—surrounded as it is with planted woods now well grown—is a pleasing object. There are walks in these woods and separate sea-bathing places for ladies and gentlemen. There is the best anchorage for yachts of the largest size close to the house." "The Inverewe gardens are wonderfully attractive, yielding as they do, exquisite flowers nearly all the year round." The following remarks about these gardens are from one of a series of letters from the Highlands which appeared in *The Times* in the autumn of 1883: "Thanks to genial winters, from the softening influence of the Gulf Stream, ornamental gardening richly repays one in those sheltered situations that slope to the sea-arms. The most enchanting spot in that way which I have seen is the garden at Inverewe, on Loch Ewe. The garden was laid out by the proprietor, Mr. Osgood Mackenzie, whose taste must be unimpeachable as his knowledge of flowers. The gardens form a terraced ampitheatre, shelving gently towards the Loch, and backed up by the hanging woods which have only been recently planted. Fruit trees but a few years old are already loaded with plums, pears, etc. The low stone walls that front the earth banks are covered with many of the rarer creepers, some of them almost semi-tropical, with luxuriant myrtles just bursting into flower and with clusters of roses of wonderful size. But what is most remarkable is the marvellous vividness of the colours in such brightly tinted flowers as crimson roses and scarlet gladioli. The warm damp seems to give a brilliancy to the tints which I have never seen, either in England or in southern Europe."

The earliest photograph we were able to discover probably dates from some time about the turn of the century. It has an interesting history. Among our visitors to the garden in September, 1960 were a Mr. and Mrs. Hugh A. Mackenzie of Toronto, Canada. He was descended, he told us, from the Mackenzies of Gairloch and had come to these parts to pay a visit to the country of his ancestors. With him in the hotel he said he had an old photograph of Inverewe which he would bring along the following morning to show us. When we saw it we were tremendously interested and he then remarked that it had been found amongst his father's effects when he died and that his father, like himself, had made a pilgrimage to the Gairloch country and had acquired this photograph at that time. My husband asked him if he would allow him to have a copy made, but, before leaving the house, he insisted on making him a present of the original (Plate 5a).

It portrays the old house, with the terrace wall and a corner of the walled garden. The trees around cannot be more than about 20 years old and here and there the outcropping rock is still visible. There is no herbaceous border, ivies have been planted against the terrace wall and there is no rock garden.

It was later that spaces were cleared for planting shrubs and fenced against deer and rabbit. Rabbits were plentiful in the garden and difficult to eradicate in the dense cover provided by Rhododendrons, until myxomatosis eventually eliminated most of them in about 1957. Osgood related that his grandfather introduced rabbits from England but "no one has suggested a monument for conferring such a benefit on the Highlands".

Most of these enclosures were sheltered with wind-resistant species. "Japan" (6 on the map) was probably the first of these to be made. No regular records of planting were kept, but a list made for this area in 1924, which is one of the few records preserved, is a remarkable account of what was tried. By 1950 the great majority of these plants had, however, disappeared. "Bambooselem" (22 on the map), one of the most sheltered parts of the garden, was made about 1903–04 and many of the original species planted still survive. The "Peace Plot" (19 on the map) was laid out in 1918–19, to celebrate the ending of the first World War.

At about 8.30 a.m. on 25th April, 1914, Inverewe House took fire and the greater part of it, except some of the rooms at the back, was burnt to the ground. The navy were in the bay at the time and, just before the fire broke out, a naval funeral took place at Poolewe. Vice-Admiral Sir Lewis Baily, Flag Commander Grant and other officers with about 800 blue jackets had come from the ships and gave much help in salvaging furniture which strewed the lawn. Osgood, who was not at home at the time, arrived on Sunday afternoon.

From this time until the house was rebuilt in 1937 the family lived at Tournaig, which was the residence of Mary, the Dowager Lady Mackenzie (Osgood's mother) till she died in 1913, and also in the lodge at Inverewe which was enlarged in 1921.

Mrs. Sawyer (Osgood's daughter) married her first husband, Mr. R. J. Hanbury before the First World War.

Osgood Mackenzie died in 1922. We never had the opportunity of meeting him, but his portrait, which hangs at Inverewe, shows a fine Highland gentleman, dignified by a massive flowing beard. He had learnt Gaelic as a child and used the language in his home and he was also fluent in French. He was a keen naturalist with an exceptional knowledge of animal life in the Highlands; he was a man of outstanding foresight and a very great gardener; a keen fisherman and an excellent shot; in fact a man of many and varied skills. As I have said many times, the garden at Inverewe will always be a memorial to him and I know of no better one that anyone could wish to have. Let us hope that it will be kept as he and his daughter would like to see it for many years to come.

As well as the National Trust for Scotland who guard it with great care there are still a number of close relatives who continue to take a personal interest in its welfare and come with their friends to visit it frequently. Of these the closest are Lady Stirling of Fairburn, Muir-of-Ord, and her daughter, Mrs. Mackenzie of Gairloch, who is now the laird, and another Mackenzie, first cousin of Mrs. Sawyer's, Mr. Colin Mackenzie, who lives in Inverness; as well as a Hanbury cousin, Lady Cunninghame-Graham, wife of the retired Admiral. When Sir Hector Mackenzie, the last laird, who was Lady Stirling's brother, died, the title had to go to his nearest male heir, but the estate was not entailed and he left it to his niece, the wife of Brigadier Stevenson. The Brigadier then took the name of Mackenzie for the sake of his wife, who had become the laird of Gairloch.

In 1962, to mark the centenary of the garden, Lady Stirling planted a small willow tree as a reminder of the only plant other than grass, heather and crowberry that was growing on the peninsula when the garden was started, and had been preserved for a long time as a curiosity. She was assisted in this symbolic ceremony by Mr. Kenneth John Urquhart, the head gardener. In April 1958 she had opened a restaurant, which we had had built, to look as unobtrusive as possible, near the entrance to the garden, and the ceremony was attended by members of the National Trust, both local and from headquarters, as well as by representatives of the Press, Transport and Hotels (by special invitation). Lady Stirling felt, as we all did, that Mrs. Sawyer would have welcomed this restaurant, because one of her great delights had always been to entertain visitors who wanted to see her garden; but she could hardly have accommodated the thousands who were then coming, in her own house. Since then the Restaurant had had to be still further enlarged more than once.

CHAPTER III

Getting to Know the Garden

It takes a year or two to know a garden really well—at all events if it is a large garden with a great variety of plants.

When we came to Inverewe in the beginning of the summer of 1954, my husband decided that it would be best to spend some time learning something about it, without in any way interfering with the general routine.

It was apparent that we might expect large numbers of visitors, some with a great knowledge of individual plants, but the great majority would be those who were interested in a more general way—in colour and in some of the lovely vistas that might be had from special vantage points—and there was no doubt, too, that much of the charm of the garden lay in the partly developed wilder woodland which contrasted so pleasantly with the more formal fenced enclosures, in which most of the more interesting plants in the garden were contained.

Before the summer had ended, it became perfectly obvious that the narrow peat paths would not stand up to an increased traffic: as soon as the surface was broken the path quickly became a quagmire in which more than one lady temporarily lost a shoe. Accordingly, during the first winter the work of path making was begun. To carry gravel by barrow was quite impracticable, because of the distance and uphill gradients. We decided to make a road wide enough for a tractor to the highest point of Ploc Ard, so that, for all the narrow paths, gravel and other materials could be dropped at convenient spots and barrowed down the slope to the place where it was required. Road making began in October, as soon as visitors disappeared, and continued throughout the winter, whenever other more urgent work allowed. Peat was removed, so that the road might have a hard foundation and a great deal of blasting had to be done in order to make the roads level and wide enough. From the scouring there was sufficient material to metal the whole surface of the road, but a good deal of work was required in making the necessary side and cross-wise drains.

From this, as a beginning, the roads throughout the garden were gradually reconstructed. By a slight alteration of alignment or by a small amount of clearing it was often possible to open up a new vista and some paths were extended so that they would reach the shore.

Another problem which demanded a good deal of attention was the continued maintenance of shelter. Gaps in the woodland area were replanted, but, where there had been a large clearing by wind-blow in 1953, replanting was confined to marginal shelter strips as it is not altogether a disadvantage to have some unanticipated clearing, if it permits of an interesting re-development.

The garden has been wonderfully planned for a succession of colour throughout the year, but there were gaps, particularly in June. Primulas and Meconopsis were certainly an answer here, though it was said that primulas would not do, and curiously enough the wild primrose was almost absent and 250 plants of it which we introduced disappeared in about two years. There was ample evidence of what could be grown successfully and, for later colour, the obvious first step to take was to increase the number of Hydrangea plants, increase the lilies, the Watsonias, the Agapanthus and so on.

My husband knew he could rely on generous nurserymen and friends for specimen plants to add interest to the policies, but it would be necessary to propagate on a

Plate 7a. *AGAPANTHUS UMBELLATUS* (3)

Plate 7b. *CHAMAEROPS EXCELSA* (6)

Plate 8. VIEW LOOKING NORTH OVER LOCH EWE (15)

generous scale; the two small greenhouses were suitable enough for raising seed; a delapidated fig house, when reconstructed, made an adequate propagation house and this was supplemented by a range of frames to which we added several more later.

The Rock Garden, which faces the severest gales, was badly needing reconstruction and this was effected during our first winter, as well as the necessary replanting of the herbaceous border—which had obviously not been done for a considerable number of years.

Many and various were the things we had to learn about this garden we had undertaken to look after, by no means the least of these being the vagaries of its climate and I shall say more of this in another chapter. But who would have thought that, in planning the day to day work in the latter part of the year, it was necessary to have two projects always on the go, so that one or other of them could be carried on, according to the direction of the wind? The cause for this?—not the force of the gale, but the smallest member of the local fauna, none other than the midge! Before going to Inverewe I had made enquiries as to what forestry workers considered to be the best protection against midge and mosquito bites and when I was told it was Mylol, I laid in a plentiful supply of it. I found it excellent myself and so did the men, to whom I gave tubes of it, but large armies of midges are sure to find a spot that has not been covered with it and it is much more satisfactory, if possible, to work where there is enough breeze to blow them away. Fortunately the Inverewe peninsula is not often without such breezes on one side or the other.

Of course the most important discoveries we had to make concerned the identity and location of the enormous variety of plants that flourished and even after we had been at Inverewe for six years we were still discovering plants we didn't know were there. This was partly due to the fact that some parts were badly overgrown and the more rampant plants were suppressing others and partly to the fact that some parts were hardly accessible until we had made paths to them through the undergrowth. Other plants could not be identified until they had flowers.

CHAPTER IV

Rhododendrons

Rhododendrons, like everything else at Inverewe, are influenced by the unpredictable climate and their times of flowering vary accordingly, but, from early March until late in June, they usually come into bloom in a continuous succession, reaching their climax in May. In a late year, however, there will not be much to be seen before late April, whilst in an early year most of the bloom is over by the first week of June; but there are always some lingerers. The late Mr. J. C. Williams of Caerhayes Castle in Cornwall used to claim that he could have a Rhododendron in flower on his dining room table every day of the year and the same thing can happen in many years at Inverewe, with plants like *R.* × "Nobleanum", *R.* "Christmas Cheer" and *R.* × Praecox flowering out of their usual seasons, as do other species erratically from time to time. But, should there be none in bloom, nothing is more decorative than the leaves of some Rhododendrons, especially those of "Sir Charles Lemon" with a rich copper-coloured indumentum on their undersides.

Each season one of the earliest species to flower in some numbers is the red *R. barbatum*, which makes a striking picture when surrounded by yellow clumps of daffodils, but, even earlier than this, I have seen the one well-grown specimen of *R. strigillosum*, its Chinese equivalent, in full flower during the first week of February. After these come species of the Heliolepsis and Triflorum series, like *R. rubiginosum*, *R. davidsonianum*, *R. desquamatum*, and *R. yunnanense*, of which there are many plants and we once saw a group of them framed by a double rainbow, making a most striking picture. They are followed by masses of yellow *R. campylocarpum* and blood-red *R. thomsonii* of which Inverewe has some excellent forms. Next, in addition to a wealth of species such as *R. fargesii*, *R. fictolacteum* and *R. arboreum*, come the hybrids, and the Rhododendron Walk is then at its gayest. The Azaleas follow, with large patches of the yellow sweetly-scented *R. luteum* and species such as *R. zeylanicum*, covered with brilliant scarlet-red flowers in July, when Primulas and Meconopsis are usually at their best. A late Azalea or two may persist and a truss of "Azor" is sometimes found in August, but, after that, there is little more Rhododendron colour until October when the leaves of the Azaleas cover some of the hill slopes with a rich red-brown.

Not only on account of their colour, however, but, also, because they reflect in a marked degree the whole history of the garden, are Rhododendrons of pre-eminent interest. Inverewe was established long after Sir Joseph Hooker had sent home seed of the "Sikkim" Rhododendrons by which gardens like Lochinch and Stonefield benefitted so much in the 1850's, and well before Wilson, Forrest and Ward had begun collecting in China, Burma and Tibet. Osgood Mackenzie acquired his first Rhododendrons about the year 1890 (there is no exact record), but presumably they were purchased and there is no doubt that Himalayan species and a variety of hybrids were the plants he chose.

From a single plant of *R. campylocarpum* many self-sown seedlings appeared in due course and this happened also with *R. barbatum*, *R. niveum*, *R. thomsonii*, *R. campanulatum* and others. Among hybrids his choice was, on the whole, for the best then available and a number of them, such as "Cornubia", "Dr. Stocker", "Doncaster", "Earl of Athlone", "Fastuosum plenum", "Gill's Crim-

Plate 9. POOLEWE FROM THE GARDEN (7)

Plate 10. RHODODENDRON LODER'S WHITE (21)

son", "Fragrantissimum", "Mrs. Henry Shilson", "Nobleanum", "Queen Wilhelmina" and "Shilsonii" carry, in the *Rhododendron Handbook*, stars denoting particular merit today. Others, on the contrary, like "Dr. Arnold W. Endz", "G. B. Simpson", "George Hardy", "Luscombe's Scarlet" and "Purpureum Elegans" are no longer considered to be worth growing. Of the last of these we were inclined to agree with this judgment, until we saw it in its setting at Inverewe, where a few plants of it are carefully placed amongst a massed group of the common yellow, sweetly scented, *R. luteum*, on a hillside which can be viewed from a distance, when both are in flower at the same time. The effect is most striking. (The "Rhododendron Walk" is marked 19 on the map.)

When extensions came to be made to the garden 20–30 years later, self-sown seedlings formed the basis of new plantings, with occasional layers from some of the hybrids. These gave the Rhododendron plantings a characteristic similarity which they continue to show today. Mrs. Sawyer explained in an article she wrote in the *Journal* of the Royal Horticultural Society in November, 1950 that the reason for this was that about 20 years earlier there had been a very bad south-westerly gale which had flattened most of the trees at the top of the Ploc Ard and it was proposed to plant the clearing with Rhododendrons instead of forest trees. People said they would never do on that exposed point, so, instead of buying new ones, they decided to try first with self-sown seedlings of the species that were already established and about 100 of these were planted.

From the earliest years of the present century, nevertheless, seed had been coming home from the various expeditions in China and, before Osgood Mackenzie died in 1922, a number of new species had been obtained from China. Amongst these, doubtless, were *R. sinogrande*, of which there is a magnificent specimen in the garden, and some of the Triflorum and Heliolepis series. But Inverewe did not subscribe to any of these expeditions and, therefore, did not secure a selection that was at all representative, nor was Osgood Mackenzie interested in raising his own hybrids. Moreover, very little interest seems to have been taken in dwarf species and only a few of these were obtained.

In 1924 Mrs. Sawyer made a census of Rhododendrons, one of the few records that have been preserved. It paints a picture, much as has been described, with under a hundred species—many of them Himalayan—and over 120 hybrids listed, a very satisfactory collection for the time. After her father's death, Mrs. Sawyer continued to plant and extend, adding new species as well as a number of new hybrids (see 18 on map). Meantime, as the Himalayan species have done, so did species of the Heliolepis and Triflorum series multiply themselves rapidly by natural sowing and spreading about the place. In addition The Royal Botanic Garden and numerous friends, with surplus plants from the Chinese expeditions, sent gifts from time to time, but while these added interest to the garden, no attempt was made to gather together species, in order that there might be a comprehensive collection of the Series as a whole and some curious anomalies thereby result. For example, though *R. wardii* is mentioned as having been planted at Inverewe, my husband was unable to find even a single plant and yet, when un-named plants began to flower, he was able to identify such comparative rarities as *R. cerasinum* of which he found two different forms, and *R. micranthum.*

From what has been said it will be clear that the picture of Rhododendrons at Inverewe has a character of its own. Unlike the comprehensive collections at places like Lochinch, Muncaster or Glen Arn and, unlike Stonefield (with which it has some affinity), with a preponderance of

Himalayan species, Inverewe stands on its own. It depends for its charm on a profusion of the best Himalayan species, together with species of the Triflorum and Heliolepis series, supplemented by a single plant (or perhaps one or two) from various series, selected as it were, at random; together with some hybrids, many of them regarded as of high merit, but undiffused by others of more recent raising and sometimes of great beauty, which have become popular in many Rhododendron gardens elsewhere.

The recent task has been to add variety by introducing species hitherto unrepresented in the Inverewe garden, particularly some of the more tender and dwarf species, as well as some of the newer hybrids. This has been done to some effect by gifts of plants from Windsor Great Park, the Royal Botanic Garden, Edinburgh, Sunningdale Nurseries, Crarae, Glendoick, The Bush, Muncaster, Brodick and some we had collected at Moffat; and by raising others from seed. But there is still a great deal of development possible in this direction.

One of the newer undertakings has been to open up an area near Camas Glas (17 on the map), one of the most sheltered parts of the garden, as a place for big-leaved species. Groves of *R. sinogrande*, *R. giganteum*, *R. magnificum*, *R. mollyanum* and *R. macabeanum* have been planted, with species of the Maddenii series in sheltered bays.

George Forrest discovered both *R. sinogrande* and *R. giganteum*. Seed of the latter he sent home in 1919 and three or four plants raised from this seeding are growing at Inverewe, although the species is rare in cultivation, because most of the seedlings that were raised perished when they were transferred to open woodland, in spite of their being given protection in sheltered bays. It flowered for the first time in this country in 1937 at Arduaine, near Oban, and my husband remembered

Lady Campbell sending the first truss to Edinburgh for him to see. Later it flowered also at Brodick and elsewhere, but the Inverewe plants, though of the same age as these others and only a little smaller, have not yet flowered. It would be an interesting plant to have well established, since it is, as the name suggests, the largest Rhododendron known: a specimen felled by George Forrest reached a height of 80 ft. and the trunk, 5 ft. from the ground, was 7 ft. 9 in. in girth. A section from this stem, the duplicate of one in the museum of the Royal Botanic Garden, Edinburgh, is on view in the Summer House at Inverewe.

R. mollyanum was found by Kingdon Ward and my husband saw it flowering for the first time at Brodick, when walking round the garden with the late Duchess of Montrose. Clearly it was a new species and he suggested to the Duchess that he should name it after her, in honour of herself and the garden, and asked her to propose a name. "Well, I am always known to my closest friends as Molly" she said. Some weeks later she wrote remarking that perhaps "Molly" was too familiar, but by that time the latin description had been written and was in the press and it was too late to make a change.

R. macabeanum was found by Sir George Watt in Manipur and he named his plant after Macabe, the Deputy Commissioner in Manipur at the time, who had helped him. The story is told of Macabe that he was the son of a coachman in the north of England and, as he was a bright boy, the squire gave him the chance of a good education. Eventually he went to Christ Church, Oxford, and passed into the Indian Civil Service. He returned from India to marry the squire's daughter, but the marriage was not altogether successful and Macabe met his end when the bungalow in which he was staying at Manipur fell upon him and caught fire as a result of the earthquake.

Other big-leaved Rhododendrons of which there are

good specimens at Inverewe are *R. falconeri* and *R. hodgsonii*, both Himalayan and familiar to us as wild plants in the Darjeeling Forests. There are moderate specimens, too, of *R. eximeum*, *R. fictolacteum*, *R. arizelum* and *R. rex*.

Brief remarks about others are called for: *R. auriculatum* has grown well, but failed to flower; *R. griersonianum*, linked with it in the same series, because of the similarity in the shape of their buds, flowers freely and is the better of being heavily pruned periodically, although not so ruthlessly as is recommended by Sir Edward Bolitho at Trengwainton in Cornwall; *R. decorum and R. diaprepes* are both conspicuous when in flower as is also *R. sutchuenense*, flowering at an earlier date and represented by many plants scattered throughout the policies. The rounded smooth leaves of *R. orbiculare* are attractive at all times of the year, but, when the plant is in bloom, more notice will be taken of its rose-pink, seven-lobed flowers, which convert the plant into a colourful mound. *R. williamsianum*, of somewhat similar habit, but on a smaller scale, is a common and very pleasing plant at Inverewe. We found, also, one plant of *R. insigne*, recognisable enough, even when not in flower, by its rather hard leaves, silvery-copper on their undersides. The lacteum series is represented by two species. The first is the Indian *R. wightii* of which there are at least a dozen good specimens, their pale yellow flowers with a crimson blotch making an attractive sight; the other is *R. lacteum*. This is the true *R. lacteum* and is probably raised from seed collected by Forrest during his 1910 expedition. When Forrest found it he thought he had discovered a new species, one that is generally agreed to be the finest Rhododendron with yellow flowers. It turned out, however, that Delavay had found it earlier. Confusion between this plant and others which were subsequently named *R. fictolacteum* and *R. galactinum* has been discussed by my husband in *George Forrest—Journeys and Plant Introductions*, published for the R.H.S. by the Oxford University Press. In her notebook Mrs. Sawyer lists this plant as No. 4254 without collector's name, but this is a wrong number. Forrest's No. 4254 was not a Rhododendron, but Wilson's 4254 which bore the name of *R. lacteum* for a time is in fact *R. galactinum.* The Inverewe plant is the true *R. lacteum* and it is interesting that it should have survived, because many of its contemporaries failed to do so. Mr. S. H. Wilding in 1921 (*Rhod. Soc. Notes*, p. 85) wrote about two plants in his garden at Stoke Poges: "They died in the most annoying way. Despite care and attention, shade and water, they slowly expired, bit by bit, first one branch, then another, then total collapse." One original plant at the Royal Botanic Garden died before the last war. The Inverewe plant is leggy and looks liable enough to expire without further vacillation, but it has been like this for many years and it may be hoped that it will continue to survive, as others have done at Blackhills, Corsock and Lochinch.

Another rather unusual plant is *R. campanulatum* var. *aeruginosum* (which is fairly common). One sees it now and again as a single plant elsewhere but not as a border to a bridle path as at Inverewe. It is about 3–4 ft. high and effective as a fringe in spring when the young leaves appear. They are, as the name suggests, of a "brilliant verdigris" colour and the undersides are covered with a whitish or pale yellow wool, which later becomes a rusty brown. As a specimen plant *R. neriiflorum* is hard to beat and Inverewe can show some good samples which are richly laden with scarlet flowers in April. *R. floccigerum*, a near relative of which "some examples are actually ugly" and which is common enough in some gardens, is represented by a single plant. *R. zeylanicum*, which I have already mentioned, is the only Rhododendron which grows wild in Ceylon, a small tree with curiously convexed leaves and it is typified by a single large specimen which dominates the Peace Plot.

Mention has been made of some of the lepidote Rhododendrons; *R. ambiguum*, with yellow flowers, spotted green, is not a showy plant, but is excellent for forming a windbreak and its growth is rapid; *R. oreotrephes* is seen at its best, planted beside a *Rhus cotinus*, where the glaucous grey and the red leaves of the two plants are in pleasing contrast. The blue *R. augustinii* we were planting among or behind groups of the yellow *R. campylocarpum*. *R. crassum*, which is listed in the Rhododendron Handbook as "D", requiring "shelter even in warm gardens inland", seems to flourish in one of the most exposed parts of the garden. A large *R. lindleyi*, however, in a very sheltered position, was killed by 24° of frost in the winter of 1954 and so was *R. dalhousiae*. Young plants of *R. taggianum* have also been killed, but *R. johnstoneanum* survives. One of the most noteworthy plants at Inverewe in this, the Maddenii series, is the hybrid *R.* × "fragrantissimum", a cross between *R. edgeworthii* and *R. formosum*, raised in 1868. They are given a sheltered position and large plants continue to flower with the utmost profusion every year. The large white, trumpet shaped flowers appear in May and for several weeks scent the whole atmosphere around them with their delicate fragrance. Another hybrid classified as "F", "usually a greenhouse shrub" is the "Countess of Haddington" which flowers freely every year in a corner that is not particularly well sheltered. There were no dwarf Rhododendrons when we went to Inverewe but we introduced several which soon flowered well, including *R. aperantum*, *R. williamsianum*, *R. pemakoense*, *R. radicans* and *R. repens*.

Although Inverewe cannot claim to possess a really representative collection of Rhododendron species and has very few of the newer hybrids, visitors to the garden are usually completely charmed with the almost unique display it provides year after year.

Since writing this chapter I have just received, on February 15th, 1964, a beautiful truss of flowers from the first tree of *Rhododendron giganteum* to flower at Inverewe and I sincerely hope that it will never look back again and that the other plants of this species in the garden will soon follow suit. This has been a very mild winter and a number of species are already in full flower at Inverewe.

CHAPTER V

Other Trees and Shrubs

As we enter the garden by the main gate the first trees we see are a number of Eucalpytus with hanging grey-green leaves, which give an exotic flare to the place. These are not the biggest Eucalypti in the place, which are nearer the house, several of them 80–90 ft. high. Our visitors, especially those from Australia, were greatly intrigued to find them flourishing naturally so far north. Many flower and fruit quite regularly and produce self-sown seedlings, but we were not able to check their identification. Osgood Mackenzie records planting *Eucalyptus coccifera*, *E. gunnii* (*E. whittingehamensis* said by Professor Henry to have narrower, less glaucous leaves and a more tapered calyx than *E. gunnii*, but now taken as a synonym), *E. cordata*, *E. pauciflora* (syn. *E. coriacea*) and *E. urnigera*.

All these are Tasmanian species (though *E. gunnii* and *E. pauciflora* also occur in Australia) and it is interesting to recall that William Anderson and David Nelson, who accompanied Cook's third expedition to the Pacific Ocean, were the first to discover Eucalyptus, when the ships Resolution and Discovery anchored in Adventure Bay not far from Hobart, on 26th January, 1777.

Since our coming to Inverewe my husband had planted about 200 Eucalyptus seedlings, a good many of them raised from seed sent to him from Australia, including the beautiful red-flowered *E. ficifolia*. The great majority did not survive, particularly those planted on the north side of the peninsula, but a few recently planted *E. pauciflora* have grown well. I tried *E. ficifolia* again in 1961, as we had a group of sturdy seedlings grown in the cool greenhouse and I was assured by Australian friends that they can stand a little frost, but the next winter was a particularly severe one and I was not able to find any of them when I visited the garden in 1962, although I had taken care to see that they were planted in well sheltered places, avoiding frost-pockets and cold winds. When Eucalyptus plants are well established frost and snow do little damage, but the tops of young plants are very often broken by gales. The large Eucalyptus tree growing below the Rock Garden was blown down by a gale in 1957, but it was jacked and braced again and now seems to be growing satisfactorily.

Among other interesting plants in the same family—Myrtaceae—which do remarkably well at Inverewe are the Chilean Myrtles. *Myrtus luma*, a tree nearly 20 ft. high, is covered with white flowers in August and these are followed by a crop of black fruits from which jam may be made. It is always a conspicuous tree because of its bark, of a striking cinnamon colour. *Myrtus bullata*, from New Zealand, grows against a wall, but does not flower. We tried *Melaleuca* and *Feijoa*, but they died.

Curiously, the Leptospermums are not as hardy as one might expect. All except one of the six or eight plants we found when we first went to Inverewe were killed the first winter we were there, during one night when we had 23° F. of frost. They were replaced and we tried a few dozen more in different situations, but not more than one or two now survive.

The Sweet Gale, *Myrica gale*, is common as a wild plant on the moors round about and it is grown in gardens for the sake of its fragrance when the leaves are crushed; it has never been specially planted at Inverewe, but there are a few clumps in the garden.

Another aromatic shrub which deserves notice is *Drimys winteri*—Winter's Bark—from South America, of which there is one plant over 20 ft. in height and others that are smaller. It flowers freely every year and does not seem to be affected by frost. It has been known since 1587 when some of the bitter aromatic bark was brought home by Captain Winter from the Magellan Straits, but it was not introduced as a living plant until 1827. The closely allied Tasmanian *Drimys aromatica*, "suitable for Cornwall and similar places" grows so easily that it has become a weed. They both belong to the Magnolia family, of which the chief representative in the garden is the genus *Magnolia* itself. There is no comprehensive collection of the species of this genus, but one or two most noteworthy plants.

Of *Magnolia stellata* from Japan there is what is "said on good authority to be the largest in existence" and given as 28 ft. high and 75 ft. in circumference. For a long time, however, it has been densely overshadowed has lost a good deal of its vigour of growth and, though it may still be the largest in cultivation, its measurements do not now correspond with the figures recorded, nor has the plant much beauty to commend it, for the flowers are out of reach overhead.

It is quite otherwise with *Magnolia campbellii* which has become almost a timber-sized tree, though not as large as specimens in the Darjeeling forest which were felled for sawing into planks for buildings. The Inverewe tree, which was planted by Osgood Mackenzie in about 1903, has reached a height of over 40 ft. and is well branched and, now and again, well budded even to the base, so much so that recently it became necessary to divert one of the paths in order to avoid sawing off a large branch. Beautiful drawings of the tree are to be found in numbers 4 and 5 of Hooker and Cathcart's Illustrations. It flowers now periodically, most often with 50–100 blooms, but in 1957 it surpassed itself, with some 800–1000 blooms; and yet some years recently it has entirely failed to produce even a single flower. The flowers come out at the end of March or early April, each one 8–10 in. across, pale pink on the outside and of a deeper rose within. So that Inverewe should never be without *Magnolia campbellii*, for which it has become so famous, we planted in 1961 another six plants which came from Brodick.

Other species of *Magnolia* grown at Inverewe include young plants of the evergreen *M. delavayi* whose large leathery leaves are resistant to wind, *M. kobus* and *M. salicifolia* and mature plants of the Japanese *M. obovata*, *M. conspicua*, *M. acuminata*, *M. wilsonii*, *M. soulangiana* varieties and *M. sieboldii*. The last of these, a bush about 8 ft. high, has most graceful white, drooping, cup-shaped, fragrant flowers, with many deep red stamens. These appear in May and often last over until July or August. *M. mollicomata* was planted but succumbed to frost.

The Lace Bark Tree of New Zealand, *Hoheria lyallii* one of the Malvaceae, is represented by specimens up to 25 ft. high, growing in sheltered positions where they are never damaged by cold winds or frost. Towards the end of June and in July its leaves, sometimes greyish, are all but concealed by an inordinate wealth of white showy flowers, each about 1½ in. across and hanging in clusters of two to five. They are succeeded by fruits which ripen, fall and give rise to a thicket of seedlings nearby. These are not easily transplanted.

Another plant in this family which does well in the open, though more usually in this country grown against a wall, is *Abutilon vitifolium* from Chile, with large pointed, serrated, cordate leaves and flowers 2½–3 in. across, of a pale lilac blue or white, appearing in May. It is, however, not a long-lived tree.

When we visited Mount Usher in County Wicklow for the first time in August 1946, we were greatly impressed by the avenue of *Eucryphia*, and yet in Mr. Walpole's book on the garden there is no mention of them. They are, of course, by no means the rarest plants at Mount Usher, but we thought they certainly deserved to be mentioned. Inverewe cannot compete with Mount Usher's exuberance, but has two plants of this genus that are well worthy of comment. The first is a very large *E. glutinosa*, planted on a slight slope with a foreground of blue *Hydrangeas*. It is some 15 ft. high and 25 ft. across and every year in August it is covered with pure white flowers, each petal, of which there are four, over an inch long, and with a bunch of numerous stamens, each having a yellow-tipped anther. The compound leaves are of a dark green, until they turn yellow before falling. The other is the hybrid *E.* × *nymansensis*, a tall evergreen column which matches in height and vigour the fine specimens at Mount Usher, and was given this name because it was first found as a chance seedling at Nymans, Staplefield, Sussex. It is a cross between *E. glutinosa* and *E. cordifolia* and it flowers in August, too, but not as freely as the others. We grew the parent, *E. cordifolia*, which is not very hardy, to a height of 8–10 ft., but the plants seldom had more than a few flowers. Young plants of *E.* × *intermedia*, a hybrid between *E. glutinosa* and *E. lucida*, raised at Rostrevor, and of the smaller-leaved *E. moorei*, from New South Wales, have made very satisfactory growth.

The family, Proteaceae, from South America and the warmer parts of Australia and South Africa, is represented at Inverewe by a few species of different genera. The Fire Bush of Chile, *Embothrium coccineum*, described by Bean as "only suitable for the mildest parts of our islands", has been in cultivation at Inverewe for 40–50 years and, although it has not reached a height of more than 12 ft., it flowers freely, though not so luxuriantly as to merit Bean's suggestion that "no tree cultivated in the British Isles gives so striking and so brilliant a display of colour as this does". Osgood Mackenzie, writing in the *Journal* of the Royal Horticultural Society of the garden in 1916, remarks that he finds few trees easier to grow and that his specimens are probably the best in Scotland at that time. The flowers are of a light scarlet, of honeysuckle shape, are produced in great numbers along the branches and are very beautiful with a favourable light shining through them.

Very like *E. coccineum* in flower and now is also grown at Inverewe are *E. lanceolatum* and the "Norquinco Form" introduced by Mr. H. F. Comber from the Andes, which flowers so magnificently at Bodnant. The two latter are much less frost tender than the former, but they all three set seed at Inverewe.

Another handsome plant—handsome for its large, shiny evergreen, divided leaves—*Gevuina avellana*—is of the same botanical family and from the same region and reaches a height of about 16 ft. Others again are the Lomatias and we grew both *L. obliqua* and *L. ferruginea*, the latter still a young plant, growing in grass as it is said to do best, but without much sign of the vigour of strength which it has at Castle Levan, near Gourock. We never saw this plant without recalling a visit my husband had in Edinburgh from the gardener from Castle Levan, when he was over 80. They had discussed its flowering and a few days later, just to show what it could do at Castle Levan, a box, almost the size of a coffin, arrived containing the top branch from one of his many trees, laden from the top to the base with racemes of brilliant mixed scarlet and golden-yellow flowers. When my husband returned the visit he was given several dozen young plants which he planted at Benmore, only seven, or eight miles away, but after the war, grass or no grass, they had all wilted away.

We tried at Inverewe some of the Banksias, the hardiest of those which grow so well on the Scilly Isles, but not with much success.

Leguminous plants do not greatly relish Inverewe's acid peat, but where the hungry, shingly soil appears and even if it is covcred with grass, as on some of the banks, Gorse or Whin and Broom (though neither are indigenous) are here and there invasive. Many of the hybrid brooms are useful for colour in the earlier part of the season, with Laburnum, followed by the yellow of the tall drooping Mount Etna Broom, *Genista aetnensis*, planted along with the Spanish Broom, *Spartium junceum*, which both flower in July. After several unsuccessful attempts the Morocco Broom, *Cytisus battandieri*, has been established and flowers well in two places and Wattle, *Acacia dealbata*, though not over happy, exists for some years, if planted from time to time. An excellent specimen of the New Zealand red-flowered Parrot's Bill, *Clianthus puniceus*, has graced one of the walls of the Lodge for many years.

A number of species of Olearia and Senecio from the New Zealand and Tasmania regions have proved to be valuable additions to the Inverewe flora—some, like *Olearia macrodonta* and *Senecio eleagnifolius*, for their wind resistance. But the most noteworthy, as an Inverewe plant, is the Chatham Island *Olearia semidentata* which has rightly been described as "the most beautiful Olearia in cultivation", distinctive because of its grey foliage and pale purplish blue flowers, growing, when at its best, into a compact bush, 8 ft. in height and 10 or 12 ft. across. It is a good plan, when there is sufficient room, to have a number of groups and that these should be of different ages, so that it is of little consequence if an odd plant dies or if a branch suddenly withers, for this is an idiosyncrasy that this species seems to possess.

Members of the peat-loving Ericaceae, other than Rhododendrons, naturally flourish. Heaths and Heathers are grown in great numbers and variety, with emphasis on the early forms of *Erica carnea*, such as Springwood White, Springwood Pink and King George for winter and spring and upon forms of *Calluna vulgaris*, such as J. D. Hamilton, H. E. Beale, County Wicklow, Tib and white heathers, including the small variety "white Mite" for late flowering in autumn, as well as varieties of the Cornish Heath, *Erica vagans*, St. Keverne, Lyonesse and others. Both the purple and the white forms of the Irish Heath, *Daboecia cantabrica*, grow well and so do species from the Mediterranean region, such as *E. australis* and its white variety, "Mr. Robert" and *E. mediterranea*, while the Tree Heather or "Bruyere", *Erica arborea*, reaches a height of 6 or 7 ft.

The Strawberry Tree, *Arbutus unedo*, reaches its full stature and flowers each year from October to December, and its relative, *A. menziesii*, the Madrona form, with its interesting copper-brown bark, has attained a height of over 20 ft.

Species of Enkianthus from Japan and the Himalayas flower freely and occasionally produce natural seedlings, but they are at their most attractive in late autumn when the foliage has turned to a vivid red or a rich brown-bronze. They were planted in partial shade and protected from severe winds, but we found them quite hardy.

Several species of Pieris are noteworthy, particularly on account of their fiery red young foliage, *P. formosa*, which attains a height of over 6 ft. and flowers in April and May and its rather hardier variety, *P. formosa* var. *forrestii*, of which Forrest collected seed while he was escaping from a monastery at Batang on the Chinese-Tibetan border. The Catholic priests, who were his hosts, were murdered when the place was set upon by neighbouring Lamas and Forrest was one of the few who got away alive. *P. japonica* is rather taller and sturdier and flowers earlier, in March and April or even February in a mild spring. Its drooping white pitcher-draped flowers are borne in long pendulous, terminal panicles, whilst the panicles of *P. formosa* are more or less erect.

Plate 11. RHODODENDRON STRIGILLOSUM (12 and 13)

Plate 12. RHODODENDRON RUBIGINOSUM (17)

One small shrub or tree from the United States that we were surprised not to find at Inverewe and introduced a few years ago was the Mountain Laurel or Calico Bush, *Kalmia latifolia*, with clusters of beautiful pink saucer-shaped flowers. It was very quickly at home in this Rhododendron garden and flowered freely.

Another genus of shrubs that have greatly increased in popularity in recent years and have made themselves at home at Inverewe is Escallonia. One hybrid that Mrs. Sawyer admired and said she would have preferred to *Rhododendron ponticum* for hedges is *E.* × *langleyensis* and I have discussed this point in another chapter. *E. macrantha*, too, has proved effective for shelter belts and does as well at Inverewe as in seaside towns in the south-west of England, continuing to bear red flowers from June to September. Inverewe can do with many more shrubs that flower as late in the season as this and, fortunately, the Slieve Donard nursery in northern Ireland has specialised in producing some excellent hybrids from the hardier species of Escallonia. The first of these to receive an Award of Merit from the Royal Horticultural Society was *E.* "Apple Blossom", with beautiful pink flowers, as its name suggests, and we established a good clump of this variety and of another one with deeper pink flowers called "Pride of Donard". These were gifts to Inverewe from Mr. Leslie Slinger of the Slieve Donard Nursery.

Characteristic of Inverewe and supplying autumn colour in a number of parts of the garden are many excellent Hydrangeas, the largest groups consisting of *H. macrophylla*, var. *hortensia* with all its flowers of the sterile, showy type, growing in a rounded inflorescene. The flowers are mostly blue because the soil is acid, but the first year we were at Inverewe we struck cuttings of some of the best forms we found there and rooted them in the walled garden, only to find them all flowering a bright pink the next year. The reason for this was that this part of the garden had been heavily limed for the benefit of the vegetables and fruit that were grown there. However, when these plants were transplanted back into the woodland garden it was not long before they produced blue flowers again. To maintain the good blue colour Mrs. Sawyer gave her plants a mulching of peat, every nine to 10 years and we continued this practice. These blue flowers are very showy from August onwards and when the weather turns cold in October they begin to change to lovely shades of greeny-blues and bluey-greens and the petals become much tougher. This is the time to pick bunches of then to fill vases in the house where they will remain unchanged all the winter and indeed, much longer if required.

There is one good group of the var. *nigra* with stems dark purple, almost black, and flowers of various shades from pink to blue, pink being the more usual colour for this variety.

Groups of the varieties of *H. serrata*, known as "Lace-caps", with an outer circle of sterile flowers surrounding a flat corymb of small fertile blue flowers, are to be seen at one end of the Herbaceous Border and, doing equally well, in much more shady places.

A very lovely species is *H. paniculata* with a pyramidal inflorescence of mainly sterile flowers, especially the var. *grandiflora*, white at first and gradually fading to pale pink, but these do not last long if picked and put into water. There is a magnificent group of them on a bank which can be seen from a distance and is reflected in the waters of the larger pond.

One plant of the strong deciduous climber, *H. petiolaris*, with outer circles of white sterile flowers surrounding small dull white fertile flowers, has climbed 50 ft. or more up a tall elm tree. It climbs by means of aerial roots, like ivy, and does not damage its host. There is another plant of it, trained so that it spreads horizontally, growing on the wall at the back of the Herbaceous Border.

We introduced a small plant of *H. quercifolia*, but it has not yet had time to flower.

In the springtime a number of good plants of Forsythia are covered with their yellow bells and *Berberis darwinii* provides a rich splash of gold, followed by the equally beautiful colour of its dark blue berries. There are numerous plants of the Flowering Currant scattered about, as if wild, and flowering in various shades of pink, deep red and white and many of these have to be ruthlessly rooted out. Less showy is the species which we introduced, *Ribes laurifolium* with smooth, shiny, rather dark green leaves, nodding inflorescences of greenish yellow flowers, followed by oval purplish black fruits.

The number of outstanding trees and shrubs to be found in the garden are too many to give here, but we have reprinted on pages 146–152 the lists of the specially interesting ones from the Guide Book to the garden, published by the National Trust for Scotland, which most visitors carry with them round the garden. I have also drawn up for this book a list of the principal plants growing at Inverewe, grouped under their countries of origin.

One particularly interesting tree of which there is an excellent specimen is the Japanese Umbrella Pine, *Sciadopitys verticillata* and another is a variegated, cut-leafed variety of the Turkey Oak, *Quercus cerris*. There are several excellent Pittosporums, the best, perhaps, being *P. tenuifolium* and its variety "Silver Queen", with charming silvery-grey foliage edged with white, and there is quite a good plant, rather over-shadowed by taller trees, of *P. ralphii* from New Zealand, with clusters of small dark crimson flowers, having stamens with yellow anthers. There is a good tree of *Davidia involucrata*, but it does not flower freely, so that its "pocket handkerchiefs",

E 2

the large white bracts, are not plentiful. The genus *Podocarpus* is represented by two natives of New Zealand, *P. spicatus* (the "Matai" or "Black Pine") and *P. totara* ("Totara") one of New Zealand's best timber trees.

The genus *Salix* is of particular interest to Inverewe, because a stunted willow was the only thing approaching a tree which was growing on the peninsula when Osgood Mackenzie bought it, and Lady Stirling planted another one in 1962 to celebrate the centennary of the beginning of the garden. This one was *Salix vitellina* var. *britzensis* which has red shoots in winter. There is a good plant of *S. vitellina*, the Golden Willow, which is kept constantly pollarded, so that it has a profusion of yellow shoots, which are particularly striking in winter before the leaves appear, and it is well placed at a bend in the Rhododendron Walk. Also well placed is a good plant of what is perhaps the most remarkable of Willows, *S. magnifica*, with broad cordate leaves, 4–8 in. long and 3–5 in. wide and purplish stems, a tree which may grow to 20 ft. in height.

We tried the Weeping Willow, *S. babylonica*, but a really good site for it had to be cleared and rid of couch grass, so that it had to be given temporary quarters high up on a hill and though it was sheltered there by other trees it may not have survived the severe winters that followed its planting.

The old Camellia tree which Osgood Mackenzie tells of having been brought from a garden in Dundonnell still covers itself in pink flowers each year and there are one or two other Camellias of about the same size, but my husband planted a number of the newer varieties dotted over a hillside and a few, such as "Donation" flowered at once in a sheltered position under trees. A number of the other trees and shrubs which Osgood Mackenzie planted died during particularly severe winters, but some have been renewed later.

On one hillside there is a large clump of very large

plants of *Rosa moyesii*, very beautiful with its dark red flowers, followed by showy long red hips in the autumn. Autumn colouring is provided, too, by a number of different species of Sorbus, none better than our native one, but *Sorbus vilmorinii* introduced by Forrest from China, is very attractive with its feathery leaves and fruits which are almost white at first, gradually turning to pink and then a deep rose-red. Another good chinese species with large brilliant scarlet fruits is *S. sargentiana* and equally good is one of the Japanese Rowans, *S. rufo-ferruginea*.

Each year we introduced new addition such as these to the flora and time will show how well they have established themselves. Many of them are the gifts of friends, especially a near neighbour, Mr. Alan Roger, who takes a great interest in the garden and brings all his house parties to see it, as do Major and Mrs. Botley from the Carron Valley who have presented many interesting shrubs to Inverewe, two very attractive ones being *Fothergilla major* and *F. monticola*, whose flowers come out, before the leaves appear, in spring, and have tufts of about 24 stamens with long white filaments which produce a "bottle brush" appearance. Their leaves provide brilliant autumn colouring, one of crimson and the other of orange-yellow. One interesting plant that Mr. Roger gave us was a climbing *Bauhinia*, *B. yunnanensis*, which unfortunately has not survived and another was a variegated variety of *Fatsia japonica* with white tips to the lobes of its leaves.

I introduced the Judas Tree, *Cercis siliquastrum*, in 1961 and it is now established, but *Liquidambar styraciflua*, the "Sweet Gum" from Eastern North America, which I had hoped would produce a brilliant splash of crimson in the autumn, succumbed to the severe weather in the winter of 1962–63. During that winter even a number of plants of the Lantern Tree (*Crinodendron hookerianum*), so much a feature of the Inverewe garden, were killed. The

Monterey Pine, *Pinus radiata*, was damaged then, too, but not killed. It is interesting to study the survey of damage suffered by plants in British gardens during that winter published in the R.H.S. *Journal* and to see how lightly Inverewe came off compared with other gardens. I was particularly interested to note that most of our new introductions had survived, although plants like the lovely *Rubus deliciosus*, with its shining white flowers like single roses, had scarcely had time to become established. It was good to realise, too, that the excellent plant of *Berberidopsis corallina* at Inverewe had come through unscathed, though it had been killed or badly damaged in a number of gardens in the south of England. It scrambles over quite a large patch of rocky ground and is very beautiful to look at, with its crimson flowers, followed by lovely coral-coloured berries, but it is not easy to handle, because of its vicious spiny-toothed leaves.

Another interesting plant of which there are now small groups and which is unlikely to be found in many British gardens today is *Olearia gravis*, for which we received seed from a friend in New South Wales, and which we had to have identified by Kew. It was originally described as *Aster gravis* by F. Mueller from specimens collected near Tenterfield in northern New South Wales and was transferred to *Olearia gravis* by Bentham in his Australian Flora.

It has a beautiful blue daisy flower and, as it is not commonly in cultivation now, it could be a special feature of Inverewe, like *O. semidentata* (which is, however, grown in other gardens in England and Scotland, though not in such numbers), and our other speciality *Primula* × *Inverewe*.

A small tree that covers itself with sweetly scented white flowers each year is *Osmanthus delavayi* and there are two of these in different parts of the garden.

There were of course, a number of Buddleias at

Inverewe when we went there, including the well-known *B. globosa*, with its yellow balls of flowers, and *B. davidi* with long drooping panicles of purple flowers. More unexpected were numerous plants of a hybrid, probably of *B. weyeriana*, known as "Moonlight", which we found rather uninteresting, because the creamy flowers with their greyish leaves are singularly colourless, but Mrs. Sawyer found it attractive because of its scent, which is certainly very pleasant and unusual. One point in its favour is that it flowers late in the season, for that is just when good colour is most wanted.

There was one medium sized plant of *B. colvilei* which has clusters of lovely dark red flowers, far larger than those of any other Buddleia in cultivation, but it was not at all happy where it was enveloped in heavy shade, which has probably grown more intense since the Buddleia was planted. It would be well worth while having another plant of it in a better setting, in half shade.

We introduced plants of two good species, *B. fallowiana* and *B. alternifolia*, which were both brought to Britain from China in 1915, and of one of the best of the newer hybrids of *B. davidi*, known as "Royal Red", whose flowers, though not really red, are of strong reddish-purple. It is impressive, growing in a commanding position on a stony hillock near the Reception Office. We had excellent plants of *B. fallowiana* in the Edinburgh Botanic Garden which were much admired by King George V and we took cuttings of it to Inverewe, where it is now flourishing and multiplying. It is a much more graceful plant than *B. davidi* and has long slender panicles of pale lavender, sweetly scented flowers, and silvery felted stems and leaves. But the most graceful of them all is *B. alternifolia* with its arching branches bearing cascades of lavender-purple flowers, though, to be seen to real advantage, it needs much more space for spreading than we were able to give it.

A small Tulip Tree (*Liriodendron Tulipifera*) which we planted seems to be growing well though it will probably be many years before it flowers.

One large tree that is particularly striking and seems thoroughly at home in a sheltered part of the woodland is *Populus lasiocarpa* one of the finest and largest leaved of poplars, which comes from China and is not often seen in gardens in this country. It has large male catkins about 4 in. long, but those that bear the fruits are much longer and, when a number of capsules burst, the tree is enveloped in clouds of white silky down, like a snow storm suddenly coming before its time.

Another rather special feature of Inverewe is a large group, almost looking like one plant, of *Desfontainea spinosa* which the uninitiated think is Holly until, in the autumn, its flower-buds begin to open into funnel-shaped flowers, with scarlet petals edged with yellow. The holly-like leaves are borne in pairs, not alternate like those of the holly.

Perhaps the "star turn" of all is the climber *Jasminum polyanthum*, which many people grow as a pot plant in the green-house, to be carried carefully indoors in the late autumn when its panicles of many fragrant white flowers will scent the house. At Inverewe it climbs the front wall of the house and its fragrance scents the room that was Mrs. Sawyer's sitting room upstairs, when the windows are opened. Its only protection during the severest winter is a glass light placed in front of the lower part of it.

We had hoped to have at least one species of *Mutisia* climbing and flowering near the front door of the House, where it would not be exposed to too much heat or much wind, but we never succeeded, though we tried more than once.

Another shrub with a sweet scent that Mrs. Sawyer must have enjoyed having outside her windows was the lemon-scented Verbena, *Lippia citriodora* and a plant of it, about 10 ft. high leant against the front wall of the house, as did more than one good Ceanothus, the lovely blues of their flowers, so rare amongst trees and shrubs, representing Mrs. Sawyer's favourite colour, like so much of the paint in the house.

On either side of the front door of the house were two neat dwarf conifers, but when one of these died, we did not replace it, planting instead the lovely *Clematis montana*, var. *rubens*, which grows fast and soon covers itself each year with lovely rosy pink flowers. The best plant of it in the garden was climbing a tall tree in the Avenue, but it had evidently over spent its strength and was perhaps, too heavily shaded, for a very strong wind one day blew it from its support and we had to cut it down. A similar fate befell a particularly good plant of *Solanum crispum*, with large clusters of bluish purple flowers like those of the potato, which was growing on a wall that had been part of the old house before it was burnt down. There are several replacements of this vigorous climber doing well in other places now. Growing against this same wall and doing well is a plant of *Garrya elliptica*, with its pendent silvery-grey male catkins as much as 6 in. long.

Very good specimens of the Everlasting Pea climbed up beside various doors, one unusual and particularly attractive one having flowers of a brick-red colour, but we never had its varietal name identified, nor did we identify all the varieties of Chaenomeles on the garden wall and on the house, one of which had flowers of a good brick red colour.

Two species of Cassinia, with white flower-heads and tawny down, occur in the garden and appear hardy there, *C. fulvida* and *C. vauvilliersii*.

A small tree that holds its own in a shaded part of the

woodland, but never seems to grow taller than about 12 ft., is *Cercidiphyllum japonicum*. Its leaves, as the name implies, are shaped like those of Judas Tree (*Cercis*) and it is for their colour that the plant is grown, deep red at first, becoming dark green, then in the autumn changing again, before they fall, to bright red or yellow. Growing in the wild in its native country, Japan, where it runs no risk of frost, it grows to as much as 100 ft. in height. Another Japanese tree that provides good autumn colour of a soft rich red and grows in a conspicuous place at Inverewe is the Nikko Maple (*Acer nikoense*) and, of course, there are a number of the better known Japanese Maples with dark red cut leaves.

All these and many more unusual and beautiful trees and shrubs mentioned in my fuller list, are well worth a personal visit to Inverewe.

CHAPTER VI

Herbaceous Border, Mixed Borders and Herbaceous Plants in General

From the terrace in front of the house we look across the Herbaceous Border, the lawn and the Rock Garden to the sea and, beyond it, to the trees and fields of the farm, with moorland and rocky hills and the mountains of Ardlair and of the Torridon Range in the far distance.

If we walk from the gate to the bend in the avenue, the length of the lawn becomes visible before us, framed, on the one side by the border which is backed by the curving terrace wall, and on the other by a bank, studded with Laburnum, *Berberis darwinii*, Sea Buckthorn, *Olearia gunniana* and Whin and topped with plants of *Adenocarpus frankenioides*, grown from seed my husband brought from Teneriffe, as far as the Rock garden of which the upper terraces are visible. Beyond this is a short hedge of *Gaultheria shallon*, about 4 ft. high, then a few clumps of blue and pink Hydrangeas, and, across the further end of the lawn, the outline of the picture is completed by a new short herbaceous border at the base of a bank which is planted with roses and brooms and overtopped by some of the largest trees in the policies—a large *Eucalyptus coccifera*, the European Silver Fir (*Abies alba*), the Douglas Fir (*Pseudotsuga taxifolia*) and large Wellintonias (*Sequoiadendron giganteum*) one of which was recently blown down in a gale. One particularly interesting plant which we had put in this new border and which should be well established by now is a most unusual Eryngium, *E. pandanifolium*, a native of Montevideo and so named because its leaves are like those of the Screw Pine (*Pandanus*), linear and pointed and very tall.

In July and August when there is more colour here than in any other part of the garden, the lawn is a favourite place for taking photographs, either of a view across the loch or of individual plants or, perhaps of the border itself, with a background of the house and the trees behind it. The steps from the lawn to the terrace on which many people liked to sit were rather surprisingly clothed with drifts of a white ever-lasting flower, *Helichrysum bellidioides*, a prostrate shrub which is a native of New Zealand and is said in this country to be half hardy and suitable for the Alpine house.

This Border is a mixed one, though mostly Herbaceous, planned to give a show of colour for as long as possible from May and June to late October. The wall behind it supports many beautiful climbing roses, vines and other climbing shrubs, such as *Hydrangea petiolaris* and, most unexpectedly, *Fuchsia cordifolia*, with green and red flowers, a native of Mexico, described in gardening books and catalogues as a greenhouse plant. I had only seen it in one other garden and that was Tresco on one of the Scilly Isles where the climate is much milder than that of Inverewe. We did cover it with branches and sometimes even a glass light for the winter, but it always survived. In front of these are the usual tall growing perennials, like the Globe Thistle (*Echinops ritro*), a very attractive foliage plant with globular heads of blue flowers, Aconites, Delphiniums, Lupins, the tall *Cephalaria tatarica* with pale yellow Scabious-like flowers, which comes from Siberia, Campanulas and Michaelmas Daises; planned so that early flowering plants are interspaced with those that flower later. Especially interesting and by no means ordinary, near the back of the border, is *Kirengeshoma palmata*, with its broad leaves and yellow bell-shaped flowers, coming out in September. It belongs to the Saxifrage family and is a native of Japan. Another plant, which gives distinction to the back of the border for a long time in the summer and autumn is the Californian Poppy, (*Romneya coulteri*) with its large, glistening white flowers, centred with striking clusters of yellow stamens.

The middle of the border is made colourful by good clumps of Phloxes, especially of a long established pink one which did particularly well, though we found the best new ones rather difficult to establish. Between the Phloxes are many old favourites such as Sidalceas, Scabious "Clive Greaves", Pyrethrums, Aquilegias, the tall white double daisy, *Chrysanthemum maximum* "Esther Read" and "Horace Read", a Sea Holly with steely blue bracts (*Eryngium amethystinum*), a good dark red Astilbe which had to be kept well watered, Heleniums, Rudbeckia, Catananche, Liatris and various species of other genera. Two plants amongst these which had to be placed with great care, because of their almost pillar-box red colour, are *Lychnis chalcedonica* and the scarlet Bergamot (*Monarda didyma*) and useful foils in front of these are the forget-me-not-blue *Cynoglossum amabile*, the dark purplish blue *Campanula glomerata* and a beautiful blue Pulmonaria, presented by Sir James Horlick who has large patches of it, established as if wild, in his wonderful garden on the island of Gigha. Behind these dazzling reds are tall blue Campanulas, especially the stately *C. lactiflora* with pale blue flowers, and the feathery white racemes of Cimicifuga or the tall stalks hung with white bells of *Galtonia candicans*, as well as the deep blues of Delphiniums and two very good Aconites, one dark and one lighter blue.

Of medium height, too, is a very attractive patch of the Ligtu hybrids of Alstroemeria, of varying shades of yellow, orange, flame and salmon pink and these have to be kept away from the patches of pink Phlox with which they would clash. Only recently established near these is a plant of the lovely yellow single Peony which is a native of the Caucasus and has the rather overpowering name of *Paeonia mlokosewitschii.* Its lustrous yellow flowers are well set off by its pale green compound leaves, of a bluish tinge, with reddish pink veins and stalks. It is a pity that people should think a name like this (and indeed many latin names) impossible and not try to pronounce it. To me it is great fun trying to get one's tongue round it; specific names of plants always mean something and give added interest to the plant, often telling of its history. This one is named after a Russian botanist who found it.

Although this is mainly a perennial border, annuals and biennials are used to produce brilliant patches of colour in the front—the well-known Nemesias especially a very good blue one of Sutton's; Petunias of many beautiful colours, *Phlox drummondii*, Candytuft, Asters and Antirrhinums, as well as some less well known ones like Arctotis, Ursinia and Dimorphotheca from South Africa and *Limnanthes douglasii* from California, which seeds itself freely and so provides patches of well advanced seedlings ready to plant out early in the Spring. Another plant which attracts much notice is *Papaver commutatum*, a striking red poppy, with large black patches on its petals, which is a native of Asia Minor and the Caucasus. We first received seed of this from the Crathes Castle garden, where it spread itself very freely.

The brilliant blue-flowered *Salvia patens* we grew almost as an annual and had good patches of it in front of the House where it could be seen to good effect.

To make it easier for our hardworking staff we were gradually replacing these annuals with short perennials, such as Pinks of various shades, Catmint, set off by good clumps of the bright pink *Viscaria vulgaris splendens flore pleno*, Heuchera, the yellow *Alyssum saxatile*, the deep pink Potentilla "Miss Wilmott", showy Erigerons, dwarf Michaelmas daises and neat little patches of a good purple

Viola called "Martin" which flowers for a long period and was a gift from its producer, Mr. Joe Elliott. More showy than this were the Swiss Roggli pansies, but we found that new plants of these had to be grown from seed each year. Patches of a small but outstanding plant, making a very good show for about three months, is *Polygonum affine*, *Lowndes' variety*, with its mass of pink flowers on short sturdy stalks, pale at first, then turning to a rich rose and finally a lovely golden brown when the flowers wither. It is much neater and has larger flowers than the type which is in the Rock Garden, and it was brought from the North-Western Himalayas by the late Colonel Donald Lowndes of the Indian Army. Many visitors asked me where it could be obtained, but I was not able to tell them of any nurseryman who had it for sale, as it was not then advertised and was given to me by Colonel Lowndes' brother. However, I have recently seen it advertised in one nurseryman's catalogue. Another delightful plant which I introduced to the front of the border was *Aster pappei*, a beautiful blue daisy from South Africa. Very showy, too, were patches of the large orange-coloured South African daisies, with brown discs (*Dimorphotheca aurantiaca*).

A very attractive grouping of plants near the front of the border and flowering late in the season, from September onwards, was *Coreopsis verticillata*, with its finely cut leaves and dainty yellow daisy flowers, contrasting with the lavender coloured single flowers of *Dahlia merckii* and a small late-flowering *Astilbe chinensis pumila*, of a pinkish lavender colour. The rose-pink trumpet-shaped flowers of *Incarvillea delavayi* borne on 1–1½ ft. stems were another good introduction to the front of the border, as were the lavender-blue broadly bell-shaped flowers of *Platycodon grandiflorum*, the Chinese Bell-flower.

With all these plants and many others we tried to keep

a good succession of colours for the whole summer, beginning with Tulips in May and carrying on into the autumn with plants of different coloured foliage, like *Stachys lanata* ("Lamb's Lugs" in Scotland, because of the white woolly leaves), *Anaphalis triplinervis*, with woolly leaves, too, and white bracts making the flower heads into "everlasting" flowers, *Senecio cineraria* and *Artemisia ludoviciana* with white or silvery grey leaves, *Lobelia cardinalis*, with dark red leaves and stalks as well as red flowers, and *Sedum maximum atropurpureum* with pink flowers in September and purple leaves. The large flat inflorescences of pink flowers of *Sedum spectabile* came in September, too, and their habit contrasted well with the mostly perpendicular lines of the other plants, as did the flat corymbs of yellow flower heads of *Achillea filipendulina*, borne on stems 4–5 ft. tall. These last can be dried and will keep their colour indoors all through the winter. Another flower which keeps its colour through the winter indoors is the annual Delphinium or Larkspur and the perennial ones do too, if picked at the right time.

Our first summer at Inverewe we wondered why there were no tulips in the border or elsewhere and we thought we would remedy this by planting large clumps of bulbs the following spring, but the experiment soon brought us our answer in the form of neat hollows in the ground where we had provided tulip bulbs for the enjoyment of the field mice. The same fate began to befall a consignment of corms of *Crocus speciosus* which I had planted in the Rock Garden, but we soon heard of Warfarin and fed the field mice with a one-in-twenty mixture of this with oatmeal. After that I always supplied this mixture when planting bulbs or corms and they were saved. Although this poison is said to be only harmful to mice and rats, I always took the precaution of putting it well inside coffee tins turned on their sides, so that other animals, especially birds, could not easily reach it. It must be renewed so that

Plate *13a*. *MAGNOLIA CAMPBELLII* (22)

Plate *13b*. *MAGNOLIA SIEBOLDII* (3)

Plate 14. "JAPAN" (6)

the mice eat it several times, but it does not cause pain to the mice, as do some other poisons which contain phosphorus.

The great merit of Tulips is that, as well as providing excellent colour groupings early in the season, they can be inter-planted with annuals or later-flowering perennials and consequently do not leave bare patches for the rest of the summer. The seed capsules should, of course, be cut off as the petals fall, so that the leaves can feed the new bulbs for the next season instead of helping the seeds to ripen. At Inverewe we found that the bulbs could be left in the ground through the winter with quite satisfactory results, though we did lift some of the best ones. The reverse process of this inter-planting we did with lilies such as *L. regale*, which we arranged to follow some early flowering perennials. An interesting new introduction to near the front of the Border is × *Solidaster luteus*, a bi-generic cross, combining the names of the two parent genera, Aster and Solidago. It has numerous small yellow flower heads.

The soil of the border is naturally very dry and stony and badly needs the help of a good mulching with farm-yard manure as well as frequent watering in dry weather, but, with this help, it is surprising to see what a wealth of colour can be produced there for so long each summer. It is fully exposed to devastating gales from the south-west, but, fortunately, these come most frequently before the plants have put on much growth, though some years they have had disastrous effects in July or August. Tying tall plants to stakes, though necessary, really ought to be so tight, to be effective, that the beauty of the plant is spoilt and it is better to take risks, especially as these plants, unlike most of the others in the garden, can easily be replaced.

As well as this main Herbaceous Border there are a number of mixed borders in other parts of the garden which combine many herbaceous plants with small shrubs and some trees and, if carefully planned, supply colour for long periods. In one such border which faces almost due west, but is not much exposed to the south-westerly winds, we had some good groups of Irises in the front, though we never tried to specialise in the newer varieties, but more showy than these were some really excellent huge flowers of lilac and white Colchicum (the so-called "Autumn Crocus") and next to them a particularly floriferous small plant of *Rhododendron pemakoense* which covered itself with pinkish flowers each year. Other small Rhododendrons in the front of this border are *R. fastigiatum* with light purple flowers and *R. russatum* with flowers of a rich violet purple and a little further back some slightly taller ones of which the first to flower is *R. mucronulatum*, which may have its early rose-purple flowers frosted, but usually has more to follow. A little later than this the lavender-blue flowers of *R. augustinii* open and then the rich crimson flowers of *R. neriiflorum*, which really prefers more shade and is much better represented in another part of the garden.

With these taller Rhododendrons are good clumps, 4–5 ft. tall, of the light blue-flowered *Campanula latifolia* and a tall Thalictrum (which we grew as *Th. dipterocarpum* though it is likely to be *Th. delavayi* with which it is often confused in gardens), with its graceful, drooping flowers having mauve sepals and clusters of stamens whose yellow anthers hang on threadlike filaments and sway in the breezes.

In the front of the border later colour is provided by the bright blue flowers of the very attractive little shrub *Ceratostigma willmottianum*, the rosy-crimson flowers of the "Bleeding Heart" (*Dicentra spectabilis*) and a smaller Dicentra with cream-coloured flowers, probably *D. cucullaria*, the "Dutchman's Breeches".

At the back of this border, next to some good blue

Hydrangeas is an interesting small tree of *Acer griseum*, with bark that peels off in flakes, revealing the orange-red new bark beneath them; and trifoliate leaves that turn to a brilliant red in the autumn.

Along one side of the avenue to the house there is almost a continuous Mixed Border providing many beautiful groupings of herbaceous plants with shrubs and trees behind them. The first part of it, near the entrance gate, is mostly covered with heaths and heathers, including some of the tall shrubby ones, such as *Erica australis*, the Spanish Heath, and its variety "Mr. Robert", with white flowers, and the Tree Heath, *Erica arborea*. With these are associated a number of Brooms, such as *Cytisus albus*, the white Spanish Broom and *Cytisus* × *praecox*, the Warminster Broom.

Further along we had planted groups of lilies, many of them new introductions from Oregon, and with them small shrubs, such as *Abelia schumannii*, with rosy pink flowers, growing singly, *Abeliophyllum distichum*, bearing clusters of white flowers with orange centres, *Weigela florida* var. *variegata*, with pink flowers and leaves edged with yellow, and a plant recently introduced to cultivation by Ludlow and Sherriff, *Euphorbia griffithii*, which has bracts of a brick orange on erect stems, about 2 ft. high. Behind these are taller shrubs, such as *Rosa hugonis* whose arching stems are covered with pale yellow single roses in May and June, followed by small dark red fruits in July and August; *Neillia longiracemosa* with long racemes of small pink flowers, rather like a shrubby Spiraea in habit; *Berberis thunbergii* var. *atropurpurea*, grown for its purple foliage; *Cotoneaster frigida*, a tall shrub with small white flowers followed by masses of brilliant red fruits, providing good autumn colour. To vary the heights are small trees, such as *Halesia monticola*, with hanging clusters of white bell-shaped flowers; *Sorbus rufo-ferruginea*, a Japanese Rowan with rust-coloured down on the undersides of its leaves, brilliant red fruits and the habit of growth of a Lombardy Poplar; and a particularly good crab apple with dark red fruits. There are, of course, many other good crab apple trees in other parts of the garden, some grown chiefly for their ornamental fruits and other for their beautiful pink flowers or dark purple leaves.

Beside the avenue, too, are large and very floriferous plants of Forsythia, showy Rhododendrons like *R. Thomsonii* and *R.* × shilsonii and a large *R. falconeri* of most unusual habit, all its branches spreading out horizontally, because its main leader was damaged at some time.

As well as the newer introductions there are large patches along the avenue of blue and white *Agapanthus orientalus* and clumps in the Rock Garden of the smaller *A. campanulatus*. Also beside the avenue and in a number of places in the garden is the flame-coloured *Watsonia beatricis* which is quite startling in its brilliance especially when lit up by the headlights of a car driving to the House. It seeds itself freely. Both of these plants are from South Africa, as is the Kaffir Lily, *Schizostylis coccinea*, which flourishes equally well in the late autumn and right on until it is cut by a severe frost. There are large patches near the house of the two varieties of this, "Mrs. Hegarty" and "Viscountess Byng", both having lovely pink flowers, but the latter variety sturdier and later flowering and of a deeper colour. They looked particularly beautiful when cut and arranged in vases with the grey leaves of *Santolina chamaecyparissus*. They are much more attractive than the rather dull white flowers of "Chincherinchee" which used to be sent to this country at about Christmas time as cut flowers from South Africa and were much appreciated at a time when there was nothing much else flowering in our gardens.

One herbaceous plant that provides one of the most

striking features of the garden is *Saxifraga peltata*, (now usually called *Peltiphyllum peltatum*) with its large umbrella like leaves, as much as 18 in. across, borne on stalks about 2 ft. high. The flowers are inconspicuous, but the leaves provide the most wonderful variety of autumn colourings in yellows, oranges and reds and at Inverewe one long walk is bordered on both sides with this blaze of colouring for over a month.

There are good patches of Astilbe, established as if wild, and a path is bordered by the Willow Gentian, *Gentiana asclepiadea*, with its almost sessile, blue bell-shaped flowers, and its variety *alba* with white flowers.

There are several good groups of Red Hot Pokers, both large and small, and a conspicuous feature of the garden is the Pampas Grass, of which there are magnificent clumps in several places.

One bank is nearly covered with Hemerocallis, the Day Lily, and these are very useful as cut flowers for the house, as are Alstroemeria and Montbretia, when they are allowed to run wild in places where they can do no damage by invading cultivated beds. They make good splashes of colour.

Another plant that is very effective covering a bank in this way is the Rose of Sharon, *Hypericum calycinum*; and there are grassy patches under trees that are covered with the pale lavender-coloured flowers of the Dog's Tooth Violet, *Erythronium dens-canis*, with its large, broadly ovate light green leaves often blotched with purple-brown and white. There are a few small groups of the var. *album* with white flowers as well as *E. americanum* from Eastern North America. We had planted several groups of the species *E. tuolumnense*, with smaller bright yellow flowers, from California.

There are, of course, many good patches of Snowdrops as well as some of the much larger Snowflake (*Leucojum hiemale*) which flower a little later. After the Snowdrops,

Snowflakes and Crocuses, of which there are not very many, come the ordinary Daffodils which cover huge areas, especially near the entrance gate, and interplanted with some of them, so as to continue the flowering period, a number of Pheasant's Eye, *Narcissus poeticus*.

Very surprisingly there are scarcely any ordinary primroses, although we introduced numbers of them and there are only small patches of the wild hyacinth.

Several areas are almost carpeted with different varieties of the wild anemone (*Anemone nemorosa*), the blue variety robinsoniana, a moderately double white variety, *alba plena*, and Vestal in which the centre of the flower is filled with broad flattened filaments of modified stamens.

We were always hoping to establish good patches of *Trillium grandiflorum*, such as we had had under trees in the Edinburgh Botanic Garden, and several kind friends from Canada or the United States were kind enough to send us rhizomes, so that we had made a beginning, and these should soon spread.

There is one large patch of Lily of the Valley plants that are very much overcrowded, but they do not take kindly to being moved. A new patch of them began to appear in another place where the overhead trees had been blown down by a gale in early 1953.

Solomon's Seal, with its white bells hanging from long bending stems with pairs of leaves along their length, is a striking plant of which there are a number of good groups.

In an area that Mrs. Sawyer called "America" in honour of the American troops who were stationed near Inverewe during the war and gave her much help in many ways, there are very interesting groups of plants in several different beds, especially Azaleas and Brooms of many colours and Lilacs. They had no special connection with America in their origin, except for one deciduous Rhododendron, though we did introduce a number of American plants there and very soon the lilies that were produced by

Jan de Graaf in Oregon became a feature of the place, especially the yellow and orange varieties, "Destiny", "Enchantment" and "Firecrown" which multiplied fast.

The area had been enclosed by wirenetting and a beautiful hand-wrought iron gate, but this became unnecessary when Myxamatosis had eliminated all but the occasional odd rabbit.

The name "Japan", too, had little connection with the origin of the plants growing there, except for one cherry tree that was sent to Osgood Mackenzie from Japan and still flourishes there though maimed by a gale which removed its crown. This enclosure is very near the sea, but it is protected by a sloping hill on one side and on the seaward side by a good hedge of trees like the New Zealand *Griselinia littoralis*, with shiny leathery leaves which can stand up to the strongest gales. Strangely enough it is in this little enclosure, so near the sea, that plants grow, such as large Tree Ferns and palms like *Trachycarpus fortunei* (syn. *Chamaerops excelsa*) which have done most to give Inverewe the reputation of being a "tropical" garden. In its shelter, too, grow many interesting and unusual plants, though they are not all particularly tender. The little Scarlet Nasturtium, *Tropaeolum speciosum*, makes a blaze of colour climbing up a Tree Fern and another chilean climber, with long scarlet pendent tubes, *Mitraria coccinea*, adorns one of the large palms and a good patch of *Philesia buxifolia* (*megalanica*) grows round another one. Here we found, too, an unusual Gladiolus called "Ackerman" of which we never succeeded in discovering the specific name. It has lovely crimson flowers borne on slender graceful stems. There is a good plant of *Paeonia delavayi*, with its beautiful deep red single flowers, and a particularly good specimen of *Meconopsis integrifolia* flowered here with several other species of Meconopsis and many good lilies.

CHAPTER VII

Meconopsis, Primulas and Lilies

As many of the Meconopsis, Primulas and Lilies are comparatively new introductions to gardening in this country, I have thought it best to give them a chapter to themselves, though it will have to be a short one, because we had only made a beginning of growing them at Inverewe and had made no attempt to have anything approaching comprehensive collections of them there.

Meconopsis

There was a woodland corner of the Royal Botanic Garden, Edinburgh, which was always a special favourite of mine. In it was a mass of *Meconopsis betonicifolia* var. *pratensis* growing behind a foreground of *Primula helodoxa*. The deep blue of the Meconopsis, with the largest flowers 6 in. across, contrasted vividly with the bright yellow of the Primula to make one of the most pleasing blends of colour that a gardener could wish to have.

Meconopsis and Primula offer for the woodland garden a wealth of varied colour and the permutations of one species with another can provide a great diversity of colour groupings. Many species of these genera flower in May, June and July and, when they are not in flower, the rosettes of leaves of some of the Meconopsis add beauty and distinction to the places where they are found. It was therefore surprising to see in more than one book on Woodland Gardening that, whilst Primulas were described in some detail, Meconopsis had not much more than scant treatment, but the reason may be that many of the species are monocarpic and so must be grown from seed each year.

We were glad to find at Inverewe clumps of *M. betonicifolia*, which had become well established perennials, and also of rosettes which seemed to be the familiar *M. wallichii*, now usually included under the name *M. napaulensis*, with either reddish, purple, blue or white flowers. When these rosettes eventually sent up their stems and flowered it was good to see that they were all—except for one or two whites—of one of the best blue forms and there were not any of the much less attractive red or chocolate. The flowers, of a lovely Cambridge blue, with each petal nearly 2 in. across, are arranged in nodding clusters on a tall stem sometimes as much as 7 ft. high. In this good blue form they are now by no means often seen in gardens.

To add to these we bought two dozen seedlings of *Meconopsis superba* and for the first two years they made fine silvery rosettes, 2–2½ ft. across, with leaves more or less deeply indented and some with a golden tinge. When they flowered they made a magnificent bed, each scape about 4½ ft. high, but the flowers, instead of being white, were yellow. There can be no doubt that this was a hybrid between *M. superba* and *M. regia* and the next generation of seedlings was much more varied in leaf colour and degree of indentation and, moreover, when they flowered, some had white and some had yellow blooms. One with white flowers attained a height of just over 8 ft.

Meanwhile seed had been obtained from the Royal Botanic Garden, Edinburgh of *Meconopsis betonicifolia* var. *pratensis* and of *M. grandis* (*Sherriff* 600) and these gave a large number of plants which, when massed as a background to Primulas, made a wonderful deep sky-blue display. The temptation to allow them to flower in their first season was too strong to be resisted and many died after flowering but they are easily raised again. They do best when there is rain in April or May, but are less robust when they are planted in places where they cannot be watered, and at Inverewe there is often a long dry spell in May. Another species which has done well from seed is *M. dhowjii* which was introduced from Nepal in 1931. The rosettes are smaller than those of other species but the deeply divided leaves often have a coppery tinge and are studded with bristles which at the base are a deep purple or almost black. The flowers, which are pale yellow, are borne on stems about 2 ft. high, and this again is a monocarpic Species. *M. simplicifolia* and *M. latifolia* have also flowered, but neither with great vigour or with any abundance. Attempts to induce *M. latifolia* to naturalise itself in the Rock Garden, as it did at one time so freely in the Edinburgh Royal Botanic Garden, were not successful, but it dislikes the rather poor soil and the gales to which the Inverewe Rock Garden is particularly exposed.

With *M. integrifolia* we had more success. This species from Yunnan flowers earlier than most and has large yellow flowers growing from the axils of the upper leaves and is a very striking plant when flowering freely. Other plants such as "Ward's form" of *M. betonicifolia* with mauve petals, *M. quintuplinervia* and the true *M. grandis*, discovered in Nepal as long ago as 1814 by Wallich, were gifts from Mr. and Mrs. Renton of Branklyn, Perth. These are all perennials and now well established.

Lastly, we were recently growing on a fairly large scale some of the new Meconopsis from Nepal, introduced by Stainton, Sykes and Williams in 1954. These somewhat resemble *M. regia* and *M. napaulensis* and have large though not compact rosettes of long-stalked, more or less deeply indented, greenish yellow leaves. The flowers vary from a light rose-pink to deep red, on scapes from 3–5 ft. high.

The Nepalese species had a particular significance for us, for we had, in our days in India, always hoped for the opportunity of going plant-hunting in Nepal and, as long ago as 1920, my husband had passed the Government of India's examination in Nepalese and one of his Forest Rangers, a keen botanist and a native of Nepal, was ready to act as guide and helper. In fact we had left India and were settled in Edinburgh before Nepal was opened to foreigners and our hope was never realised.

Primulas

Very few Primulas used to be grown at Inverewe and, in talking of this to an old friend of Mrs. Sawyer's we said we had heard that she thought they did not like Inverewe and would not do well there. The friend's reply was "yes, but I believe the dislike was mutual"! Be that as it may, it was abundantly clear that, if suitable sites were chosen, the more vigorous Primulas, like some of the candelabras, would be sure to flourish. Colour throughout the garden was badly needed in June and July, when most of the Rhododendrons were over, and Primulas were one obvious answer to the need. This called urgently for large-scale planting in many places, for example near the ponds, below the outcrop of pink Torridon sandstone, on the fringe of some of the ditches, at strategic points by road junctions and here and there along the sides of paths. A first experiment was made by dividing the plants in a small bed of *Primula pulverulenta*—a good strain of clear reddish purple—and this we quickly followed by dividing such other plants as were available and securing seed of other species. We soon had a large patch of *P. pulverulenta*, looking particularly beautiful below a cliff of Torridon sandstone when a shower of rain has made the colour of the sandstone a deep pink.

Primula helodoxa was there in some quantity, growing with *P. florindae* in thick tall grass by the edge of a drain.

It well justified its name "The Glory of the Marsh" having golden yellow flowers, arranged in a candelabroid inflorescence, and it has grown exceedingly well in dry as well as in damp places. It seeds freely and the seed is pure, as it does not cross with other species. When more seed was collected than was needed for sowing in prepared places, the surplus was scattered on freshly turned ground where a new path had been made. However, attempts to naturalise this and other species in this easy manner were not successful. Seedlings of Foxglove (which were not sown) arose in great numbers, only to be swamped before long by an overgrowth of couch and oat grass. Altogether a good deal of broadcast sowing of the most robust species was done, with the aim of producing primula-strewn glades as at Logan in Wigtonshire, but with no success except for one small patch of some 30–40 seedlings of *P. helodoxa* which appeared through the grass, after an interval of three years.

P. japonica, usually the most vigorous of the Candelabra section, never produced more than an odd self-sown seedling, though it is, of course, easily raised from seed and by division and of this species there are now a large quantity at Inverewe, in various forms—pink, white and dark red, the very pale ones not very attractive, but one of the best for colour being "Miller's Crimson". *P. japonica* does not need as moist a situation as many of the candelabroid Primulas.

Already in the garden were four or five plants of a beautiful candelabroid hybrid whose origin is unknown. We heard that an old gardener came to visit Inverewe and, after being shown round by Mrs. Sawyer, he remarked: "You have some very beautiful and interesting things, but I have a Primula which you haven't got and I'll send you one." This one plant had produced the small clump, which we found when we went to Inverewe, of plants producing flowers on stems 2–3 ft. high and borne in five to eight tiers, of a rich bright red-brick hue. It may be a hybrid of *P. pulverulenta* and reminds one of the hybrids "Red Hugh" and "Lissadel" but is a much more robust plant and has larger flowers than either of these. It did not set seed, so we began at once to increase it by division and soon had a massed planting, set off by patches of the yellow *P. helodoxa* and a background of the blue *Meconopsis betonicifolia*. My husband had seen nothing quite like this plant elsewhere and we decided to call it *Primula* "Inverewe". It appears to be quite sterile, but, even if seed were produced, it is unlikely that it would breed true. However, it reproduced vegetatively very fast and numerous patches of it throughout the garden have become a special feature of Inverewe. The sites for it have to be chosen with care, because of its bright colour which clashes badly with any pink flowers, such as late-flowering Rhododendrons or the pink forms of Meconopsis.

Other Primulas of the Candelabra section planted on a large scale include *P. bulleyana*, a tall growing plant, with scapes often 2 ft. high, bearing orange-yellow flowers, and hybrids in various shades of yellow, orange and pink, as it crosses very readily; *P. prolifera*, with yellow flowers, introduced in 1954 from Nepal by Stainton, Sykes and Williams; *P. cockburniana* which is short-lived though seed is plentiful. This last is the smallest member of the Candelabra section, seldom more than 18 in. in height, but it has several tiers of orange-red flowers. It does not need as much moisture as the other members of this section, though it does need a fairly rich, moist soil and some shade. Another small member of this section and one of the least common which did quite well with us is *Primula aurantiaca*, with rich coppery flowers and, as the flowers develop, the scape leans over and bears a rosette of leaves, which will form a new plant when it reaches the ground. *P. pulverulenta*, which I have already mentioned as one of the few Primulas we found at Inverewe, is perhaps the most robust of this section and at Inverewe it multiplies very freely with masses of self-sown seedlings which we were able to transplant to almost any situation, where we wanted a massed planting and quick flowering in newly developed parts of the garden. The older plants can be divided for quick multiplying as well as growing it from seed. Its variety known as "Bartley Strain" because it was produced by Mr. G. H. Dalrymple of Bartley, has fine pink flowers and we planted good patches of it. Unlike the "Inverewe" cross this strain is now fixed and can be grown from seed. For early flowering in March and April the well-known and easy to grow *P. denticulata* has been planted in large groups in various colour forms from lilac to crimson and, for later flowering, *P. mooreana*, with its capitate inflorescence of deep lilac-blue flowers which come out in late July, August and September, is particularly good for Inverewe, supplying colour in the woodland when it is much needed. It can be propagated by division as well as from seed.

Some of the Sikkimensis Section, with the flowers in umbels at the ends of the scape, have lent themselves to fairly extensive planting, though it was difficult to find damp enough places for large drifts of them, especially for the most outstanding of them all—*P. florindae*, which likes real bog or at least the banks of streams or ponds and will even grow in shallow water, but needs plenty of shade as well. Our small groups of it, growing in drains beside some of the paths, made a good show, but really large colonies are much more effective, though these need a real water garden and better feeding that we were able to give them with mainly crumbly peat. Our plants, even in the wettest places we could find for them, never grew to the giant size usual in many other gardens, where their almost round heart-shaped leaves have stalks as much as a foot in length, and the flower scapes may be 3–5 ft. in height. *P. florindae* was only introduced to British gardens in 1924 by Kingdon Ward, but it has been one of the most popular primulas ever since then. It is easily raised from seed, of which it produces large quantities, and by division as well.

Some other members of the Sikkimensis Section have lent themselves to extensive planting at Inverewe: *P. sikkimensis* itself, with neat tufts of leaves and yellow campanulate flowers borne by a scape 1–2 ft. in height, which produces many self sown seedlings and likes damp places in woodlands; *P. secundiflora* which might almost be a smaller version of the last one, having smaller and more glossy leaves and purple flowers; *P. alpicola* with pale yellow flowers and its varieties *alba* (white) and *violacea* (violet-coloured), all three heavily dusted with yellow farina. *P. alpicola* was found by Kingdon Ward at high altitudes in south-eastern Tibet and, although it likes plenty of moisture, it needs a fairly well drained soil and it is suitable for a place in a Rock Garden if it can have some shade and be supplied with plenty of leaf-mould or peat. We did not try them in our Rock Garden, which is exposed to fierce drying winds and has very poor stony soil.

Two small Primulas that I did try to establish in the Rock Garden, though without much success, were *P. farinosa* and *P. frondosa*.

P. farinosa is wild in Scotland and England and in South America and there are large colonies of it in the Lake District of England, but these are in damp upland meadows and it obviously likes more moisture than I was able to give it, even with frequent spraying. A more plentiful supply of leafmould would help to keep its roots moist whilst the flowers are enjoying the full sun. It is a very attractive little Primula and well worth persevering with. It is called the "Bird's Eye Primrose" because its flowers, which vary in colour from light purple or lilac to pink and even white, always have a yellow eye. The flowers are borne in compact heads and, as the name suggests, are densely powdered with white farina, as are the undersides of its leaves.

P. frondosa resembles *P. farinosa*, but it is larger and not so neat and compact. The scape and the undersides of its leaves are densely powdered too, but its flowers are more purple. It is a native of the Balkans, but it grows among damp rocks and needs to be planted in soil that does not dry too easily.

Both these Primulas seed freely, but the seedlings of *P. farinosa* are very difficult to handle, because their roots are very fine and easily damaged.

With such a small number of gardeners, we made no attempt to grow the more difficult species of Primula or to strive for a representative collection, as some flower too early to be appreciated by visitors, who do not come in numbers before the middle or end of March. But we had fair success with *P. nutans*, *P. chionantha*, *P. sinopurpurea*, *P. capitata*, *P. bracteosa*, *P. viali*, *P. poissonii*, *P. calderiana* and *P. melanops*, though some of these are not very robust and may be short-lived, so that fresh batches of them have to be grown from seed each year. *Primula viali* is perhaps one of the most outstanding of the genus and is well worth the care that must be lavished upon it, seeing that it is supplied with a rich compost, moderate shade and plenty of moisture during the growing season. Its farinose scape carries a spike of flowers which are a deep violet blue when fully out, but scarlet in bud, and the whole effect is like a small "Red Hot Poker".

Neither *P. forrestii* nor *P. sonchifolia* have been, as yet, successfully introduced, in spite of several attempts made by us.

Some of the finer Auriculas have been tried, but have a short life, possibly because of a deficiency of lime, but the Polyanthus varieties do well. Of these last we had seed of

Plate 15a. *MECONOPSIS BETONICIFOLIA* (6)

Plate 15b. *MECONOPSIS INTEGRIFOLIA* (20)

Plate 16a. *RHODODENDRON BARBATUM* IN "PEACE PLOT" (21)
Plate 16b. IRISES AND SMALL POND (8)

a special New Zealand strain and a patch of this made a very good show, but they were not really any better than Sutton's best strains and not as good as some of Blackmore and Langdon's which we introduced later, especially their blue one.

Lilies

None of the Lilies are so comfortably at home as to have naturalised themselves at Inverewe, as they have done occasionally elsewhere, but there are enough to add colour and distinction to the garden when they flower, between May and September. Among those which grow freely are some of the commoner species like the purple and white varieties of *L. martagon*; the Tiger Lily (*L. tigrinum*) with nodding, scentless, fire-red blooms; the Leopard or Panther Lily (*L. pardalinum*) orange or orange-red, spotted with crimson-brown; the Lily from the Pyrenees (*L. pyrenaicum*) yellowish with black spots and with a strongish odour to which most people object, so that it is of no use as a cut flower, and the large nodding, pale yellow, bell-shaped flowers of *L. szovitsianum* from the Caucasus. There are, also, some attractive yellow and deep red forms of the Umbel Lily, now under the general name of *L. × hollandicum*.

More attractive, however, than any of these is the Regal Lily (*L. regale*) of which there are numerous clumps in various beds, including the Herbaceous Border. It stands from 2–4 ft. high and has large, very fragrant funnel-shaped flowers, up to 6 in. in length, rose-purple on the outside, white inside, with a yellowish blotch in the throat. It is easily raised from seed and by this method the stock was being steadily increased. It has been in cultivation for a much shorter time than the others mentioned, having been discovered by Wilson in Szechwan in 1903.

The Golden-rayed Lily of Japan (*L. auratum*) had been

common at one time at Inverewe, but had died out, probably through a virus infection. We introduced it again some years ago and now it seems to be well established once more. It grows as high as 7 or 8 ft. and bears on its rigid purplish green stems many large, golden-streaked, crimson spotted flowers, late in August and in September, October and even November. In fact there were often a number of buds still unopened at the end of November and these I used to pick, for fear of damage by frost, and take into the house, where they continued opening for some weeks.

Amongst the most vigorous Lilies in the garden are the Bellingham hybrids of which there are numerous groups which have been established at Inverewe for a good many years. These hybrids are a batch of plants which were raised in about 1918 by pollinating *L. humboldtii* with pollen from *L. pardalinum* and *L. parryi* at Bellingham in the State of Washington. They are very tall, growing to a height of up to 7 ft. and bearing some 12–20 orange or yellow, red- or brown-spotted, turkscap flowers, which, according to their colour, have been given distinctive names. These names have long ago been lost from the Inverewe plants, but they probably include "Frances Larrabee" with deep yellow flowers, "Mercer Girl" and "Vashon" of the light yellow flowered varieties.

During recent years we introduced from America and Canada some of the new and wonderfully vigorous hybrid lilies from the Jan de Graaff Bulb Farm in Oregon and we were very successful with some of the "Mid-Century Hybrids" which were raised by crossing upright lilies of the *L.* × *hollandicum* type with pollen of *L. tigrinum* and with further hybridisation to produce such types as "Destiny", a pure lemon-yellow lily with a few brown spots on the petals providing a beautiful contrast. They grow on stems nearly 3 ft. tall, carrying some six to eight open flowers above the dark green foliage. Others which have done well are "Enchantment", a similar lily with nasturtium-red flowers, and "Firecrown" with flowers of a deeper shade. We tried as well as these "Ruby" "Pink Perfection" and "Royal Gold" but these did not multiply fast.

Some of the Aurelian Hybrids (raised by crossing *L. henryi* with a trumpet lily) and of the Olympic Hybrids make a fine show in July, when the bloom of *L. regale* is past. These and others with which we experimented at Inverewe seem to multiply fairly rapidly.

The Giant Lily from the Himalayas (*Cardiocrinum giganteum*) has been growing at Inverewe for a long time and, also, its dark-stemmed Chinese variety *yunnanense*.

In the peaty soil, which is apt to become hard in dry weather, these lilies do not reach a height of 10–12 ft. as they do at Crathes and elsewhere, but, even on stems 6–8 ft. tall, these long trumpet-shaped, fragrant, drooping flowers are much admired in several corners of the garden. The rosette of large, glossy, cordate leaves is attractive even before the flower-stalk appears and, after the flowering is over and the seeds have been scattered the tall stalks bearing the opened capsules make a distinctive and beautiful decoration in the house.

Nomocharis

There is really very little difference between the genus *Nomocharis* and *Lilium* and some species could well be placed in either genus, though they are still kept separate.

We grew several species of Nomocharis from seed, but attempts to establish them on a large scale failed and a few dozen plants were all we could produce in the short time that we had tried them. The most handsome of these is *N. mairei*, a plant which grows to 2–2½ ft. in height, with a head of several large, open, almost flat, white or pinkish, orchid-like flowers with drooping stalks. The inner segments of this species are broadly ovate or orbicular, fimbriate on the margin and speckled with reddish purple spots. Rather like it is *N. pardanthina*, with the purple spots confined to the lower third of the segment, but our seedlings did not come true to type, showing every degree from unspotted to deeply spotted, variation in breadth of segment and considerable difference in fimbriation. We had a few plants, also, of *N. souliei* with single flowers of deep crimson maroon. This species was named in honour of the French missionary, Jean André Soulie (1858–1905) who was murdered by Tibetan monks at Paan (Batang).

We found a very well established and overgrown group of the Scarborough Lily, *Vallota speciosa*, with brilliant red flowers, which we tried to divide, but it took a long time to settle itself after moving. It is a native of South Africa and belongs to the Amaryllis family, but its almost regular perianth makes it look more like a lily—hence its common name.

Another very beautiful and unusual flower we found growing in long-established groups was a dainty red Gladiolus which had been given the name *Ackermannii*, but we were not able to discover its specific name or its place of origin, though this might be done with a little more investigation.

CHAPTER VIII

The Rock Garden

The Rock Garden was built from stones which formed part of the old mansion house, a series of narrow terraces with parallel paths above and below, joined by a wide steep stairway. What soil there is, even with a top dressing, is of poor quality and the whole area is exposed to the fiercest southerly winds (see 5 on map). It is therefore, not an easy place in which to grow plants and one is amazed to find how many tender exotics do manage to adapt themselves to these conditions. Mrs. Sawyer herself said it could hardly be called a rock garden, but was a real "Russian salad of plants", though it held a "good many treasures" and this it certainly does.

When we went to Inverewe many of the walls were on the point of falling down and some had already collapsed, so that complete reconstruction was necessary and this we undertook in the early part of our first winter there. The general structure was not altered, but it was extended to include a massive projection of natural rock, from which we cleared the soil and grass, and the lower path was prolonged at one end by steps to the lawn and at the other end, westwards past the boathouse, to make easy access to other parts of the garden. Two new winding transverse paths with steps make inspection and planting easier. Surplus stone we deposited at the foot of the large rock and, as it was so near the sea, we thought it worth while experimenting with some seedlings of *Myosotidium hortensia* (syn. *M. nobile*) which obviously disliked the formal beds in which it had been planted. A barrowful of earth made pockets amongst the stones and the plants were transferred to this new site. Though it provides them with little sustenance and they are fully exposed to the wind, they have grown, flowered and seeded remarkably, encouraged by an occasional mulching with seaweed and, now and again, a handful or two of fish meal to take the place of decaying sharks which they enjoy in their natural habitat. A covering of branches protects them from the worst gales and cold air during the winter months.

Seed from various sources, particularly from the Royal Botanic Garden, Edinburgh, and the gifts or occasional purchases of plants enabled us to re-stock the Rock Garden. We took care, of course, to preserve the plants that were there, especially the larger and more valuable ones, such as a large patch of a prostrate Juniper, good specimens of *Teucrium fruticans*, *Fabiana imbricata*, *Escallonia rubra pygmaea* and three large plants of *Cistus* × *cyprius* which flowered freely, though some years later two of these three plants were killed in a particularly severe winter of gales and it was noticeable that the survivor was growing where it was sheltered by trees from the prevailing south-westerly wind. It continues to flower freely, as does *Cistus* × *Silver Pink* which we introduced later. At one end of the Rock Garden a large bed of *Crinum* × *powellii*, which produces numerous white or reddish, trumpet shaped flowers every year, we left undisturbed. There was also a small patch of *Rhodohypoxis baurii*, with white or rose-red flowers, which still does fairly well, but has to be covered with a cloche for the winter, partly in order to keep it from getting too wet. Another interesting plant which we left undisturbed was *Carmichaelia enysii* which had formed a compact mat of flattened branches.

Among the more recently introduced species and genera which have settled down in this unkindly environment I might mention the Moroccan *Anacyclus depressus* which spreads flat on the ground, turning up its white fronted and purple-backed flowers to be admired. Several Campanulas, as well as those that were there earlier, have grown well, such as *C. aucheri*, *C. barbata*, *C. raineri*, *C. carpatica* and some of its varieties. The New Zealand *Celmisia hookeri* which is regarded as difficult to cultivate, is well established and its rosettes of silver-coloured pointed leaves make an interesting diversion against a low wall. We were surprised to find no Cyananthus, but there are now good patches of *C. lobatus* and *C. integer*, but *C. sherriffii* we tried more than once, without managing to keep it alive during the winter, even under a cloche. The red-flowered *Delphinium nudicaule* from California, and the blue *D. tatsienense* from Szechuan are interesting innovations and doing well, though we grew them almost as annuals, producing new plants from seed each year. One or two species of Codonopsis are quite at home, too, as well as several varieties of *Phlox subulata* and a more recent introduction, *Phlox stolonifera* "Blue Ridge", which was given to us by Mr. E. H. M. Cox of Glendoick, Perth, who had collected plants in Asia with Reginald Farrer.

Hybrid Gazanias of South African origin make handsome patches of colour in the Rock Garden and elsewhere—yellow, white, orange and purple—in the later part of the season, but these are not hardy enough to be left out for the winter and cuttings are made each year and put in a cold frame or cool greenhouse. A beautiful clump of *Mesembryanthemum* "Penzance Pink", looks quite at home on the large rock, but it, too, has to be taken in for the winter, though it very quickly flowers again when brought out in the spring. A very different *Mesembryanthemum* which attracts a great deal of attention on account of its brilliant, rather garish, mixture of colours is the much more ordinary "Livingstone Daisy" which we grew each year and planted out in patches to make a bright display near the entrance to the garden, but not in the Rock Garden.

Attempts to grow Gentians have not been very successful in the Rock Garden except *G. septemfida* which is an old inhabitant. The white-flowered *G. saxosa* from New Zealand did well at first, but, after one of the two best plants had been appropriated in full flower by an unknown visitor, we preferred to grow it in another part of the garden. Even the "climbing form" of *G. sino-ornata* which was given to us by the late Mr. Norman Webster of Knockmie, near Forres, as one of the easiest to grow, prefers a more peaty bank where it is now doing extremely well. The typical *G. sino-ornata* is established fairly well in other parts of the garden, including the new rock garden, Creag a Lios, where a beginning has been made with various other species.

The well-known Edelweiss, *Leontopodium alpinum*, which vandals have now made scarce in some parts of the Swiss Alps, made itself at home with us, though I hasten to say it came from plants bought from a nurseryman! *Ramonda myconi* has taken kindly to growing in cracks in the walls, as well as *Lewisia howellii;* and *Erinus alpinus*, with either white or purple flowers, is well established in many crevices and multiplies freely from self-sown seeds.

Various species of Tulip, Narcissus and Crocus have multiplied well and the dwarf *Iris innominata*, which was introduced from Oregon in 1936, is a useful species which increases and flowers freely, with either yellow or blue flowers. I planted a number of corms of *Crocus speciosus*, although it is said to spread like a weed in some gardens, but the mice did not give it a chance until I supplied them with Warfarin, and, in any case, its spread is limited by the size of the small stony pocket, and the same applies to *Crocus tomasinianus* and *Crocus vernus* which flowers for several months. I was given a particularly good variety of the latter, called "Harlem Gem", by Mr. Evan Cox.

Here, as well as in other parts of the garden, there are masses of the "Pygmy" *Narcissus asturiensis*, a native of Portugal and Spain, as well as groups of the "Hoop Petticoat", (*N. bulbocodium*) and *N. cyclamineus*, with deep yellow, reflexed segments, and these are planted in the Rock Garden along with the blue and white *Chionodoxa luciliae* ("Glory of the Snow") and the striped Squill (*Puschkinia scilloides*). Another grouping of ours, which many visitors found attractive was the scarlet *Tulipa eichleri*, surrounded by blue Grape Hyacinths.

Polygonum affine and *P. vaccinfolium*, both from the Himalayas, are useful mat-forming plants, with rose-red or pale pink flowers continuing late into the season. Lowndes' variety of the former, with compact cylindrical heads of darker red flowers, we transferred to the front of the Border, in our drive to replace annuals with low growing perennials there.

Perhaps the most interesting introductions to the Rock Garden are *Linaria alpina*, both the type with bluish violet flowers and var. *rosea* with pink flowers, *Salix* × *boydii* (found as a new discovery on the Berwickshire hills), the dark red-leafed Knaphill form of *Rhus cotinus*, *Caryopteris* × *clandonensis*, with grey leaves and light blue flowers, and the prostrate form of *Cotoneaster frigida* which creeps along the ground and has no spectacular merit until autumn, when each little shoot is richly covered with ripe red berries. Plants of *Daphne retusa* proved too attractive to some knowing visitors and were removed, but one plant is now doing well. Two other attractive shrubs which provide a contrast to the many low-growing alpines are a neat little plant of *Olearia nummularioflia* and one of *Veronica hulkeana*, with the protection and support of a wall behind it.

One rather interesting plant in the Rock Garden which none of our visitors seemed to have seen elsewhere is a double form of *Meconopsis cambrica* with deep orange flowers, which, being double, do not seed, unlike the type which is one of the most persistent weeds to be found anywhere. I have recently found one nurseryman's catalogue which mentions the double form.

Another plant, newly introduced, which made itself very much at home in the poor soil is *Jasione jankae* from Hungary, with heads of blue flowers on long stalks, looking at first sight rather like a small scabious, though quite unrelated and belonging to the Campanula family.

Silene schafta has made good patches and its pink flowers are particularly valuable because they come out from June to October, when most Rock Garden flowers are over. *Saponaria ocymoides* covers one large pocket and would spread further, its rose-pink flowers continuing for most of the summer.

There are good patches of Aethionema and Androsace and good carpeters, like *Potentilla fruticosa* var. *arbuscula*, more prostrate than the type and covered with yellow flowers for most of the summer. *Hypericum olympicum* and its variety *citrinum*, with pale yellow flowers, and two small Primulas, *F. farinosa*, with lilac or purple flowers, which grows wild in several parts of England and Scotland and one very like it, *P. frondosa* with rose-lilac flowers, from the Balkans, which I have mentioned in another chapter.

One or two small Rhododendrons, such as *R. campylogynum*, hold their own here and even flower well some years, but much better situations can be found for most of them in other parts of the garden, one exception being *R. aperantum* which seems to have found a spot to suit it and covers itself with flowers each year. Heaths and Heathers, such as *Calluna vulgaris* "H. E. Beale" and "J. H. Hamilton", are, of course, a great feature, especially in the autumn, but space is limited here and we planted much larger patches of Heaths and Heathers in several other parts of the garden.

The Harebell Poppy, *Meconopsis quintuplinerva*, is just

holding its own in a very stony pocket and thrives on a little extra feeding.

Several small pinks like *Dianthus alpinus*, *D. neglectus* and *D. deltoides* made good little patches in the crevices between stones on the paths and the steps.

Brunnera macrophylla, with its little forget-me-not flowers, needed no encouragement to make large patches in the stoniest places and a daintier plant of the same family which was equally at home was *Omphalodes cappadocica*.

The native Scottish plant *Dryas octopetala* soon made itself at home, as did the Rose Root, *Sedum roseum*, and *Silene acaulis*, the Moss Campion, with stemless pink flowers, which, however, was not spreading at all well, as in the wild.

The "New Zealand Sheep," *Raoulia australis*, did not take long to establish itself and spread into a large patch, but a flat one, and it would have looked more like a sheep if I could have planted it on a hillock. Another New Zealand flower which I grew was interesting rather than attractive, *Craspedia uniflora*, with a single flower-head on tall stalk, having no ray-florets, only bright yellow disc florets on a globose head. Another very different New Zealand plant which was spreading was *Acaena glabra*, an unusual plant, with numerous spines, belonging to the Rosaceae, and somewhat similar in habit to our Salad Burnet, with small globose heads of flowers.

I have already mentioned the new rock garden, to which we gave the Gaelic name of Creag a Lios, (this is marked 9 on the map) and it is quite different from the other Rock Garden. It had been started by Mrs. Sawyer who says of it in the Guide Book "most of the soil and peat had been stripped away to lay bare an attractive buttress of red sandstone". We had the stripping continued to expose more of the sheer face of this magnificent Torridon sandstone and, at the foot of it, we much enlarged a bed of a good deep pink *Primula pulverulenta* which produces masses of seedlings each year. When these Primulas are in flower this becomes one of the most spectacular corners of the garden, especially when a good shower of rain has emphasised the colour of the lovely red sandstone. Earlier in the year it is very beautiful when framed from above by the pink and white and purple of Triflorum Rhododendrons, *R. davidsonianum*, *R. yunnanense* and *R. rubiginosum*.

Many small plants have been tucked into the crevices of the rock and into a few small terraces made below it, as well as beside a new set of steps at one end where, amongst other things, *Rhododendron yakusimanum* and *R.* "Elizabeth" are quite at home. One interesting plant doing well here is the very small *Gunnera magellanica* which shows us one of nature's striking contrasts when we compare it with its close relation *Gunnera manicata* whose enormous rhubarb-like umbrellas are the largest leaves in the garden. Another is the New Zealand plant, *Ourisia macrophylla* with showy white flowers.

Another even more impressive outcrop of rock was later cleared above the low path on the north side of the peninsula and a loose scree of rock, that was mostly produced by blasting to make new paths, was spread out below the bluff to finish it off naturally. On this scree, which is sheltered by trees and shrubs between it and the sea, a number of heathers of different varieties, small rhododendrons, brooms and other rock plants are now established and it will soon be clothed, to contrast with the perpendicular rock which we wished to keep clear of vegetation. One striking plant we did put on this rock is *Schizophragma hydrangeoides* and this shows to great advantage in this position.

Rock is not far from the surface in any part of the peninsula so that the whole of it is really a glorified Rock Garden and the surprising thing is that so many large trees manage to hold their own on it, their roots often forming little more than a close mat. It is no wonder that scarcely a winter passes without a smaller or larger number of them being blown down.

White Heather Fund

So great was the desire of visitors to carry away sprigs of white heather which they saw growing in the garden that we thought we might as well supply the demand and, at the same time, provide a source of income for the introduction of new plants. Accordingly, we decided to sacrifice one frameful of well-rooted cuttings which were actually in flower and launch a "White Heather Fund" to raise money for the purchase of urgently needed equipment. We put up a notice in the reception office saying that visitors who wished to take away a memento of Inverewe might have one of these little plants in a pot, if they would give a donation of 5*s*. or more to the Trust. Each morning about a dozen of these rooted cuttings were transplanted into little composition pots and taken to the office and so immediate was the response that it was not long before a further supply of them was needed. Before the season was over we had disposed of all the plants we had available and received in return the remarkable sum of £64 5*s*. 8*d*. The subscription list was headed by a particularly generous one of £5 5*s*. from a London lady who had lost a diamond brooch which had been found in the garden and returned to her.

The next year we had prepared a larger number of rooted cuttings to meet the demand and we were rewarded with £79 3*s*. The following year the sum rose to £103 15*s*. 11*d*., this time including the product of the sale of surplus seed collected from plants of special interest, such as Meconopsis and Primulas, which many visitors had seen for the first time at Inverewe and were anxious to have in their own gardens. To help them I wrote a few cultural instructions and had copies of these typed and given to those who bought the seed. This most useful sum of money was used for the purchase of a Trewhella Monkey Winch.

Wishing Well

Another human whim made the old copper water butt at the foot of the Rock Garden assume the role of Wishing Well, into which children, both young and not-so-young, dropped their coins. Not often were they persuaded that silver might be more effective than copper, but, by the end of the season, over £4 had accumulated. The next year this function began earlier in the season and provided us with £17, almost all in coppers, which we used for buying Rock Garden and other plants. Of course in a real wishing well the money is not removed, but, in a shallow open water butt it would have been too tempting for very young children if it had not been removed frequently. Moreover, it supplied an ever-increasing income for the enrichment of the garden flora and many young friends were entertained by helping to count the pennies.

The old water butt began to have holes which made it impossible to fill it more than half full and we soon had to scrap it altogether, but it would have been a pity to deprive children of the fun they had dropping pennies into it, as well as the garden of a source of income for buying plants, so we looked around to see how we could replace it. The ever resourceful Kenny John remembered an old copper boiler that had become rubbish, but, as this looked even less like a Wishing Well we decided to build stones round it and in this way we made it quite impressive. We then had to devise a means of lifting the boiler out, so that we could remove the pennies from time to time and the income from this source increased every year.

Mrs. Sawyer would have added her coins to the rest, for her wishes for Inverewe have gone on being more and more amply fulfilled.

CHAPTER IX

Aristocratic Weeds

It has been said of the Dandelion that, if instead of being a common native weed, it were a rare and exotic plant, its advent to cultivation would have been hailed with acclamation. This raises the question: "What is a weed?" One well-known dictionary has the definition as "any useless plant of small growth", but there are many useless plants of small growth which we do not regard as weeds but cultivate with care and, moreover, a weed may be neither small nor useless. It is really a plant that has invaded a place where it is not wanted and at Inverewe this definition can be applied to many plants that are offered for sale at high prices in nurserymen's catalogues and generally described as being most beautiful and attractive.

Like every woodland garden, Inverewe has places where the ground is not under direct cultivation and which it would be a mistake to keep too tidy and in these places the number and variety of exotics that appear is remarkable. In *A Hundred Years in the Highlands* Osgood Mackenzie mentions seven Himalayan, Chinese, Chilean and New Zealand plants which in his time were spreading rapidly and in the chapter in the revised edition written by his daughter, Mrs. Sawyer, many more are added to the list. It would seem that this aristocratic weed flora does tend to change from time to time and, in recent years, this may be due partly to an excess of tidiness demanded in a garden where very large numbers of visitors come annually; partly to improvements and extensions calling for the removal of unwanted intruders; to the desire for plants by purchasers or friends or to the use of these for new plantings, but the following census records the position at the present time, excluding those that regenerate casually and not in considerable numbers. One of the most prolific is *Pernettya mucronata*, the "Prickly Heath", which seems to be as much at home in the acid peat of Inverewe as it is round the Magellan Straits of South America where it has its origin. As a garden plant, Bean describes it as "one of the finest ornamental berry-bearing shrubs we have". It spreads very rapidly by suckers, forming dense low thickets and here and there extending to some hundreds of square yards. Wherever there is a piece of open ground it may be expected to appear as a solitary bush or to start a new colony, where seed has been dropped by birds. It dislikes dense shade. Plants vary in height from 1–4 ft. being nearly prostrate or erect and drooping, and, with their small evergreen hard spiny leaves, short, red-striped shoots and minute bell-shaped flowers, they are attractive even in summer. But it is in autumn and winter that it is most valuable, when the bushes are laden with berries—pure white, white tinged pink, crimson, purple or a dark ruddy brown, varying in size from that of a small pea to a small cherry. They bear fruit intermittently and sometimes so freely that the small shrubs are laden to the ground. Some people say that birds seldom touch the fruit; that was not, however, our experience. Blackbirds were particularly fond of them, possibly at a time when there was little else for them to find, and they often stripped certain patches, usually beginning with the white berries, but they generally left enough to see us through the winter, and well into the spring. As the berries are full of small hard seeds the appetities of the birds ensure a rapid spreading through the garden.

Another ericaceous plant which spreads by suckers in a similar manner is the "Partridge Berry" (*Gaultheria*

ate 17a. *CRINODENDRON HOOKERIANUM* (SYN. *TRICUSPIDARIA HOOKERIANA*)
LANTERN TREE (6)

Plate 17b. *DESFONTAINEA SPINOSA* (14)

Plate 18. SYN. *PELTIPHYLLUM PELTATUM SAXIFRAGA PELTATA* (19)

shallon). It fruits freely—dark purple berries about three eighths of an inch wide—and the fruits are eaten by birds, but it does not spread about all over the garden like the Pernettya. Well established clumps, however, increase fairly rapidly and if it is to be kept under control, it is advisable to cut it over with a scythe about once a year. It then forms a close-knit carpet, but where it had been left for more than two years, the woody shoots became too hard for control by the scythe and eradication became a major operation. It grows quite well in the open, attaining a height of 4–5 ft., but it is an ideal plant for a shady place, surviving even under the dense shade of a beech. The leaves are large, rounded and bristletoothed and the egg-shaped flowers, on terminal racemes 2–4 in. long, of an attractive pinkish white are often admired, especially where plants have been allowed to become woody and form an excellent short piece of hedge along part of the lawn, near the end of the Rock Garden.

Less of a weed, because it spreads only by suckers from an originally planted clump, is the well known "Rose of Sharon" (*Hypericum calycinum*). Allowed to spread where there is room, it has made dense low carpets either in partial shade or in the open, covered more or less freely, from June to September, with large yellow flowers.

Of plants dispersed throughout the garden by the agency of birds, *Drimys aromatica* is the most remarkable. This Tasmanian plant—an evergreen of the family Magnoliaceae—is a shrub up to 12 ft. high and is very attractive, with its smooth dark green pepper-flavoured leaves—and its red shoots and petioles. Although it is said to be "suitable only in Cornwall and similar places", it is found abundantly here and there in sheltered and shaded parts of the Inverewe woodland. The flowers, each half an inch across, give the plants a certain distinction when they appear in April and May and these are followed by terminal and axillary clusters of black or deep blue fruits. They have been used as a substitute for pepper and their pungent taste seems to appeal to the local birds. There is no record of when the first plant was introduced to Inverewe but it is not difficult to find several hundred seedlings, at various stages of development, grouped together in different parts of the garden.

Another species which behaves in the same manner is the well known *Berberis darwinii* which has been described as being "in the very first rank of garden plants". Following a wealth of orange and golden flowers, which appear in April and May, come the deep blue-black fruits in summer and early autumn, much enjoyed by the bird population who scatter the seeds about the garden. Young plants arise usually on earthy slopes devoid of peat, but, if they are to be allowed to survive, they must be left where they are, as only very young seedlings can be safely transplanted.

About as prevalent as the common Rowan (*Sorbus aucuparia*) which comes up everywhere, is the Chinese Rowan (*Sorbus vilmorinii*) a small tree of 12–15 ft. which was first raised by Vilmorin from seed received from the missionary, Delavay, in 1889. There are some half dozen mature specimens of this species in different parts of the woodland, the finest of them by Craig a Lios, and it is easily distinguished from the other species by its small elegantly divided leaves and, after flowering in June, by its usually heavy crop of whitish to rosy red fruit in autumn. These fruits are eagerly sought after by birds and seedlings crop up frequently even in densely grass-covered areas.

Two Himalayan Cotoneasters, *C. acuminata* and *C. simonsii*, both with red fruits, are distributed in a similar manner, the first usually in half shade and the other anywhere in the garden.

The Chilean myrtle (*Myrtus luma*) of which we had a plant over 20 ft. high until part of its crown was broken off in a gale, is a conspicuous feature on account of the cinnamon-brown colour of its bark. There is still enough crown left on this tree to flower freely and the white flowers are followed by black fruit. Numerous seedlings appear within 50 yds. of the parent and occasionally further from it, but it does not spread about the garden, as do the other plants I have mentioned. These seedlings are difficult to transplant successfully.

One of the most useful shrubs from the point of view of shelter is the New Zealand *Griselinia littoralis* and, although Bean records that "it is rarely seen in fruit in this country", it regenerates from seed quite freely at Inverewe. Its glossy green foliage is very attractive and, if plants are wanted for hedging or planting elsewhere, it is usually possible to pick up 30–40 seedlings and with care these can be moved safely, even when they have reached a considerable size. There are a few plants of a very attractive variegated form with green, and white leaves, but we never found seedlings of this.

Another plant which behaves in a similar manner, as far as regeneration is concerned, is the Chilean *Crinodendron hookerianum* (*Tricuspidaria lanceolata*) which is often called the "Lantern Tree". It derives this name from the large crimson urn-shaped flowers, 1–1½ in. long, which hang from the tree in May and June. It is perhaps a shrub rather than a tree for numerous branches often arise from near the base of the plant. The largest specimen in this garden, which attained a height of over 25 ft., was 93 feet in circumference before it was badly damaged by a large beech tree which fell on it in a recent gale, but it is shooting from the base again.

I should, also mention a compact group of seedlings, covering several square yards, of the beautiful New Zealand "Lace Bark" (*Hoheria lyallii*) in a position not very far from one of the parent trees. The seedlings are, however, so densely crowded that they are not easy to transplant.

A number of plants, of course, owe their easy distribution to the lightness of their seeds, which are readily carried by wind and this applies to various shrubby Veronicas, but only one *V. salicifolia*, falls into the category of a weed. It is attractive enough, if kept under control, an evergreen, 4–6 ft. high bearing from July onwards its small flowers, which are usually white, on racemes 4–6 in. long. It appears naturally on rather dry ground in somewhat shaded positions, in one place almost obscuring a very fine bank of *Mitraria coccinea*.

Most conifers do not reproduce naturally at Inverewe—seedlings of *Pinus sylvestris* are not common within the policies, but they occur in considerable numbers on waste open moorland immediately to the north of the policy woods, a favourable position with regard to the wind. Within the policies seedlings of Lawson's Cypress (*Chamaecyparis lawsoniana*) are rather plentiful in one or two positions, and here and there throughout the policies self-sown specimens of the decorative Western Hemlock (*Tsuga heterophylla*) may be found.

Of Rhododendrons a goodly number regenerate themselves with considerable freedom and this is true of some of the first to be cultivated at Inverewe, like *R. campylocarpum*. Plants of this species, now established in more recently planted parts of the garden, are, as Mrs. Sawyer tells us in the illustrated guide to the garden, the offspring of the original plant which occupies a dignified place in the "Peace Plot". A great number of them are now quite mature and many are congregated near the View Point and by the lower path which makes for Camas Glas and, when these are in flower about the end of April, they give an immense charm, especially when viewed from the shelter hut above. They vary in colour from a deep yellow to a pale shade, almost white, and some of the best forms my husband used to say are as beautiful as any he had seen.

With them and in other parts of the garden are plants of *R. thomsonii* which likewise are descendants of one or two original introductions and amongst these are forms which connoisseurs like to pick out and admire.

Other Himalayan species, *R. barbatum*, with its tightly packed scarlet trusses and spiny-petioled leaves, and *R. niveum*, the best specimen large-trussed and of a royal deep purple, are the descendants of early plantings and are also common about the place.

A number of Chinese species have multiplied themselves in the same way, particularly *R. ambiguum*, *R. yunnanense*, *R. neriiflorum*, *R. rubiginosum*, and *R. sutchuenense*, the flowers of one of the last, a remarkable plant, richly suffused by rose. And finally I should mention *R. ponticum*. Whether or not it can classify as an aristocrat, it is emphatically one of the most troublesome weeds.

These are not the only Rhododendrons that regenerate naturally. Mrs. Sawyer, in the supplementary chapter she appended to the last edition of *A Hundred Years in the Highlands* mentions also *R. decorum*, *R. griffithianum*, *R. cinnabarinum*, *R. eximium*, *R. falconeri*, *R. fictolacteum* and *R. sinogrande* and these may still be found, but now scarcely in sufficient quantity to justify their inclusion in a list of weeds. My husband did, however, take from the top of a single moss-covered stump nearly a hundred seedlings of *R. zaleucum* of which there was then only a single parent plant. In giving this list Mrs. Sawyer was adding to a list of seven exotics mentioned by her father which behaved in this way. It is interesting to note that two of these seven should now be excluded from the census. One of these, *Cassinia fulvida* (*Diplopappus chrysophyllum*) is not now spreading, though the position of some plants in the garden suggests that they were self-sown. Of the other one, *Leycesteria formosa*, there was no trace at all, until we re-introduced it, and this is unusual for this particular plant, because it has a bad reputation for spreading in many other gardens where it has been grown. Her own list includes others which I have omitted because one finds now only isolated seedlings—Olearia, Pittosporum, *Eucryphia glutinosa* and Eucalyptus; but the aristocratic nature of Inverewe's weeds is undoubted.

CHAPTER X

Plants and Where They Come From

With such a gloriously varied gathering of plants growing happily together like old friends of Inverewe, it is interesting to remember that they did not always live together and, in fact, most of them are "in-comers" to Scotland and there is scarcely a country in the world that did not contribute to the magnificent display. Our gardens and gardeners owe a great debt to these countries and an even greater debt to our intrepid explorers who brought these trophies back from their often very dangerous travels in remote parts of the world. As this is a book about a Scottish garden, we cannot fail to pay a special tribute to a very great Scotsman, George Forrest, a native of Falkirk, educated at Kilmarnock Academy in Ayrshire, who gave our gardens a completely new look by quite literally risking his life in unbelievable ways. My husband edited his *Journeys and Plant Introductions* for the Royal Horticultural Society and woodland gardeners should read it if they do not know it already. In it the late Professor Sir William Wright Smith, F.R.S., who was Regius Keeper of the Edinburgh Botanic Garden, tells of Forrest's first journey to Western Yunnan, in 1904, for Mr. A. K. Bulley of Neston in Cheshire and of his experiences when he was the guest at one of the French Missions there. "The Chinese were having one of their periodical disputes with the Tibetans, and the latter did not discriminate between Chinese and other foreigners and were massacring Chinese and French missionaries with equal zest. Forrest was at Tseku as a guest of Père Dubernard, a veteran of the French Mission. A party of 80 (including Forrest and his 17 collectors and servants) had hurriedly to evacuate Tseku and flee. Overtaken by the pursuing Tibetans, all were killed except a bare dozen. Père Dubernard was brutally tortured to death and a fellow priest killed on the spot. Of Forrest's personal following only one survived. Forrest had the good fortune to escape 'after a pursuit of some 10 days without shelter and practically without food'."

That was the first of eight journeys that Forrest made, based mainly on Yunnan and Szechuan, which were never again fraught with such danger, as the country became relatively quieter. "But Forrest's personality contributed to good relations. He was soon on friendly terms with the Chinese, with the Tibetans, and with the tribesmen of many names."

He collected no less than 30,000 botanical specimens from Yunnan, his choice being quite general at first but gradually concentrating more and more on trees and shrubs and especially Rhododendrons, while "Primula was never forgotten."

My husband, who contributes the chapter on Rhododendrons, says, "Among those who during the present century have added to our knowledge of the flora of Upper Burma, Tibet and Western China, and who have greatly enriched our gardens by hundreds of plants from those regions, Forrest shares the honours with Wilson, Farrer, Rock and Ward. As far as the genus Rhododendron is concerned, however, it will readily be allowed by all who know his work and who enjoy his plants, that there he reigns supreme."

Of his last journey in 1931 he wrote in a letter home: "I may with safety say that this will be the best year I have yet had. If all goes well, I shall have made a rather glorious and satisfactory finish to all my past years of labour." Little did he know that his years of labour really were at an end, for on 6th January, 1932 when the heavy work of the expedition was almost finished and the time of his departure for home had nearly come, sudden death from heart failure came to him after he had been out shooting near Tengyueh. He is buried in the graveyard there, side by side with his old comrade Consul Litton who died after their adventurous journey together in 1906. I can think of no better end that could have come to a man like George Forrest, who loved above all the wide open spaces.

With this thought in mind it seemed to me a good idea to study the lists of some of the principal plants growing in the garden at Inverewe, sorted out under their places of origin. The result will not surprise those who have large woodland gardens of their own, though each has its own special characteristics; but perhaps a little enlightening to those who still think of the north of Scotland as almost arctic in climate. Most of all I hope it will prove useful to those wise people who are hoping to find a refuge from the world of "city centres", "fly-over" roads, and flats in buildings mounting skywards and may even be fortunate enough to find this refuge in the north-west of Scotland. They are offered a selection of plants of tried stamina that have made themselves at home on a rocky peninsula often swept by fierce gales, but one thing they must remember is that these plants have enjoyed a lime-free peaty soil and a climate with no great extremes of temperature, though there is no certainty that they must have these conditions. In fact George Forrest, who had made quite a considerable study of Geology as well as of Botany, had found that many Rhododendrons do grow in a limey soil and the same applies to many other plants in this list.

EUROPE

Abies alba	Central and South
"European Silver Fir"	
Acanthus mollis var. *latifolius*	Italy
Andromeda polifolia minima	Arctic Europe and Asia
Aquilegia alpina	Switzerland
"Hensoll Harebell"	
Campanula cochlearifolia	Mountain areas
,, *garganica*	Italy
,, *poscharskyana*	Dalmatia
,, *raddeana*	Caucusus
,, *raineri*	Switzerland
Cercis siliquastrum	South
Cistus palhinhaii	Portugal
Clematis alpina	North
Coronilla emerus	Central and South
Cyclamen neapolitanum	South
Cytisus albus	Spain, Portugal and
"White Spanish Broom"	North Africa
Daboecia cantabrica	South-west
Daphne blagayana	Yugoslavia and Austria
Dianthus alpinus	Austrian alps
,, *neglectus*	South-west
Erica arborea	Caucasus and North Africa
,, *australis*	Spain and Portugal
,, *mediterranea*	South-west
Erinus alpinus	West
Erythronium dens-canis	and Asia to Japan
Genista aethnensis	Sicily
"Mount Etna Broom"	
Genista pilosa	South
,, *sagittalis*	South-east
Gentiana acaulis	
,, *asclepiadea*	
Heleborus corsicus	Sardinia and Corsica
Hypericum olympicum	South-east and Asia Minor
Iris reticulata	Caucasus
Jasione jankae	Hungary

Laburnum alpinum "Scotch Laburnum"	South
Laburnum anagyroides "Common Laburnum"	South
Lavandula spica "Common Lavender"	
Leontopodium alpinum "Edelweiss"	Switzerland
Lilium pyrenaicum	Pyrenees
Linaria alpinum	Switzerland
Lithospermum diffusum	Pyrenees
Morisia monantha syn. *M. hypogaea*	Corsica and Sardinia
Myrtus communis	South to Asia
Narcissus bulbocodium	Spain
,, *cyclamineus*	Portugal
,, *asturiensis*	Spain and Portugal
Primula frondosa	Balkans
Prunus laurocerasus "Cherry Laurel"	East and Asia Minor
Pterocephalus parnassi	Greece
Rhododendron hirsutum	
Rhus cotinus	South and Caucasus
Rosmarinus officinalis "Rosemary"	South and Asia Minor
Santolina chamaecyparissus var. *nana*	South
Scabiosa lucida	South
Scilla peruviana	Mediterranean
Senecio cineraria "Sea Ragwort"	South (naturalised in Britain)
Spartium junceum	Mediterranean and Canary Islands
Sternbergia lutea	Central
Teucrium fruticans	South
Veronica gentianoides	Caucasus
Viola jooi	South-east
,, *saxatile* var. *aetolica*	South-east

AFRICA

Canary Isles

Adenocarpus viscosus	Teneriffe

Madeira

Orchis maderensis

Morocco

Anacyclus depressus	
Cedrus atlantica var. *glauca* "Atlantic Cedar"	Atlas Mountains
Cytisus battandieri	

South Africa

Agapanthus orientalis	
,, ,, var. *albus*	
Buddleia auriculata	
Dierama pulcherrimum	To Transvaal
Dimorphotheca aurantiaca	
Gazania nivea	
Melasphaerula graminea	
Nerine bowdenii	
Rhodohypoxis baurii	
Schizostylis coccinea "Kaffir Lily"	
Tritonia crocata	
Vallota speciosa	
Watsonia beatricis	
,, *wilmaniae*	

AMERICA

North America

Aquilegia caerulea	Rocky Mountains
,, *longissima*	Texas to Mexico
Arbutus menziesii	British Columbia to California

Arctostaphylos × media	Washington
Callirhoe involucrata	Central U.S.A.
Camassia fraseri	Middle
Camassia leichtlinii	West U.S.A.
Clethra alnifolia "Sweet Pepper Bush"	South-east U.S.A.
Delphinium nudicaule	California
Erythronium americanum	East U.S.A.
Erythronium tuolumnense	California
Fothergilla major	South-east U.S.A.
,, *monticola*	South-east U.S.A.
Garrya elliptica	California and Oregon
Gaultheria shallon	West from Alaska to South California
Halesia monticola	Central U.S.A.
Iris cristata	East U.S.A.
,, *innominata*	Oregon
Kalmia latifolia	East U.S.A.
Leucothoe catesbaei	South-east U.S.A.
Lewisia cotyledon	California
,, *howellii*	Oregon
Lilium pardalinum	California
Limnanthes douglasii	California
Mahonia nervosa	British Columbia and California
Peltiphyllum peltatum syn. *Saxifraga peltata* "Umbrella plant"	California
Penstemon roezlii	West U.S.A.
Phlox adsurgens	California
Pseudotsuga taxifolia "Douglas Fir"	British Columbia southward
Ribes saguineum "Flowering currant"	North-west U.S.A.
Rubus deliciosus	Rocky Mountains
Sequoiadendron giganteum	California
Taxodium distichum	South-east to Mexico
Trillium grandiflorum	
Yucca gloriosa	South-east U.S.A.

Central America

Beschorneria yuccoides	Mexico
Choisya ternata	Mexico
Cestrum purpureum	Mexico
Fuchsia cordifolia	Mexico
Salvia patens	Mexico
Tigridia pavonia	Mexico

South America

Abutilon vitifolium	Chile
Asteranthera ovata	Chile
Azara petiolaris	Chile
Berberidopsis corallina	Chile
"Coral Plant"	
Berberis darwinii	Chile
Cortaderia argentea	
syn. *Gynerium argenteum*	Temperate South America
"Pampas Grass"	
Crindodendron hookerianum	
syn. *Tricuspidaria hookeriana*	Chile
"Lantern Tree"	
Desfontainea spinosa	Chile and Peru
Drimys winteri	
Embothrium coccineum	Chile
,, *lanceolatum*	
Escallonia macrantha	Chiloé Island
Eucryphia cordifolia	Chile
,, *glutinosa*	Chile
Fabiana imbricata	Chile
Fuchsia magellanica	
Gevuina avellana	Chile
"Chilean Nut," "Chile Hazel"	
Gunnera manicata	South Brazil
Jovellana violacea	
syn. *Calceolaria violacea*	Chile
Libertia formosa	Chile
Lippia citriodora	Chile
"Lemon or Sweet-scented Verbena"	

Mitraria coccinea	Chile and Chiloé
Myrtus luma	Chile
Nothofagus obliqua	Chile
,, *procera*	Chile
Oxalis adenophylla	Chile
,, *enneaphylla*	Patagonia and Falkland Islands
Passiflora caerulea "Passion Flower"	Central and Western South America
Pernettya mucronata	Magellan and Chile
Philesia magellanica syn. *Philesia buxifolia*	Chile
Solanum crispum	Chile
Tropaeolum polyphyllum	Chile and Argentina
,, *speciosum*	Chile and Chiloé

AUSTRALASIA

Australia

Acacia dealbata "Silver Wattle"	also Tasmania
Callistemon citrinus	
Dicksonia antarctica	
Eucalyptus gunnii	also Tasmania
Eucryphia moorei	
Olearia gravis	

New Zealand

Acaena glabra
Aristotelia racemosa
Arthropodium cirrhatum
Bulbinella hookeri
Carpodetus serratus
"Putaputawheta"
Carmichaelia enysii
Cassinia vauvilliersii
,, *fulvida*
Celmisia hookerii

Clianthus puniceus
"Parrot's Bill"
Coprosma propinqua
Cordyline australis
Gentiana saxosa
Griselinia littoralis
"Shining Broadleaf"
Helichrysum bellidioides
Hoheria lyallii
Leptospermum scoparium
var. *Nichollsii*
Libertia ixioides
Myosotidium hortensia syn. *M. nobile* Chatham Islands
Nothopanax arboreum
Olearia haastii
,, *macrodonta*
,, *nummularifolia*
,, *semidentata* Chatham Islands
Ourisia macrophylla
Phormium tenax
,, *tenax purpureum*
,, *tenax variegatum*
Pittosporum colensoi
,, *eugenioides*
,, *ralphii*
,, *tenuifolium*
Podocarpus spicatus
"Matai" or "Blackfire of N.Z."
Podocarpus totara
Ranunculus lyallii
Raoulia australis
Senecio elaeagnifolius
,, *laxifolius*
,, *rotundifolius*
ronica hulkeana

Tasmania

Billardiera longiflora
Drimys aromatica

Plate 19. *CAMPANULA RAINERI* IN ROCK GARDEN (5)

Plate 20. THE LARGE POND (14)

Eucalyptus coccifera
,, *cordata*
,, *urnigera*
Olearia gunniana

ASIA

Bhutan

Primula bracteosa
Rhododendron eximium

Burma

Meconopsis betonicifolia
Primula helodoxa
Rhododendron aperantum
R. burmanicum
R. calostrotum
R. magnificum — also Tibet
R. taggianum

Ceylon

Rhododendron zeylanicum

China

Acer nikoense — also Japan
Arundinaria nitida
Bergenia delavayi
Buddleia alternifolia
,, *fallowiana*
Caryopteris tangutica
Ceratostigma wilmottianum
Chionodoxa luciliae — Asia Minor (and Crete)
Clematis armandii
Clethra delavayi
Cornus kousa
Cotoneaster dammeri
,, *horizontalis*
Cynoglossum amabile
Daphne retusa
Davidia involucrata

Delphinium tatsienense	
Forsythia suspensa	
Gentiana sino-ornata	also Tibet
Hydrangea paniculata	also Japan
,, *sargentiana*	
Iris chrysographes	
Jasminum polyanthum	
Ligularia clivorum	
syn. *Senecio clivorum*	
Lilium giganteum var. *yunnanense*	
,, *tigrinum* var. *splendeus*	
Lonicera tragophylla	
Magnolia delavayi	
,, *wilsonii*	
Neillia longiracemosa	
Osmanthus delavayi	
Paeonia delavayi	
,, *lutea*	also Tibet
Picea likiangensis	
Pieris formosa var. *forrestii*	
Populus lasiocarpa	
Primula aurantiaca	
,, *beesiana*	
,, *chionantha*	
,, *bulleyana*	
,, *cockburniana*	
,, *melanops*	
,, *nutans*	
,, *poissonii*	
,, *pulverulenta*	
,, *secundiflora*	
,, *sino-purpurea*	
,, *viali*	
Rhododendron ambiguum	
R. argyrophyllum	
R. arizelum	also Burma and Tibet
R. augustinii	
R. auriculatum	
R. auritum	

R. basilicum	
R. bullatum	
R. callimorphum	
R. calophytum	
R. campylogynum	also Burma and Tibet
R. camtschaticum	
R. chryseum	
R. ciliicalyx	
R. concinnum	
R. crassum	
R. davidsonianum	
R. decorum	
R. desquamatum	also Burma and Tibet
R. diaprepes	also Burma
R. dryophyllum	
R. fargesii	
R. fastigiatum	
R. fictolacteum	
R. floribundum	
R. fortunei	
R. fulvum	
R. giganteum	
R. glischrum	
R. griersonianum	
R. habrotrichum	
R. haematodes	
R. heliolepis	
R. hippophaeoides	
R. impeditum	
R. insigne	
R. irroratum	
R. lacteum	
R. lutescens	
R. mallotum	
R. meddianum	also Burma
R. micranthum	
R. neriiflorum	
R. orbiculare	
R. oreodoxa	

R. oreotrephes	also Tibet
R. racemosum	
R. roxieanum	
R. rubiginosum	
R. russatum	
R. russotinctum	
R. sidereum	
R. sinogrande	also Burma
R. souliei	
R. stewartianum	also Burma and Tibet
R. strigillosum	
R. sutchuenense	
R. trichocladum	
R. wardii	
R. williamsianum	
R. yunnanense	
Rodgersia aesculifolia	
,, *pinnata*	
Rosa farreri var. *persetosa* "Threepenny Bit Rose"	
Rosa hugonis	
,, *moyesii*	
,, *omeiensis* var. *pteracantha*	
Roscoea humeana	
Rubus tricolor	
Salix magnifica	
Sorbus hupehensis	
,, *sargentiana*	
,, *vilmorinii*	
Stranvaesia davidiana	
Thalictrum dipterocarpum	
Trachycarpus fortunei	
Viburnum henreyi	
,, *rhytidophyllum*	
,, *tomentosum* var. *mariesii*	also Japan
Weigela florida var. *variegata*	

Himalaya

Androsace primuloides

Anemone obtusiloba var. *patula*
Buddleia colvilei
Clematis montana rubens
Cotoneaster frigida
Cyananthus lobatus
Delphinium himalayense
Euphorbia griffithii
Jasminum officinale
Microglossa albescens
Polygonum amplexicaule
  ,, *vacciniifolium*
Potentilla arbuscula
Primula capitata
  ,, *denticulata*
  ,, *involucrata*
  ,, *rosea*
Rhododendron arboreum also Ceylon
R. arboreum var. *roseum*
R. arboreum var. *cinnamomeum*
R. barbatum
R. campanulatum
R. campbelliae
R. campylocarpum
R. ciliatum
R. cinnabarinum
R. cinnabarinum var. *roylei*
R. cinnamomeum
R. dalhousiae
R. elliottii
R. fulgens
R. falconeri
R. glaucophyllum
R. grande
R. griffithianum
R. hodgsonii
R. hookeri
R. lanigerum
R. lindleyi
R. maddenii

R. manipurense
R. megeratum
R. niveum
R. thomsonii
R. triflorum
R. wightii

Japan

Acer japonicum
,, *palmatum* vars.
atropurpureum, *septemlobum*
Astilbe simplicifolia
Berberis thunbergii var.
atropurpureum
Camellia japonica
Cercidiphyllum japonicum
Chaenomeles japonica
"Maule's Quince"
Chaenomeles lagenaria
"Japanese Quince"
Elaeagnus pungens var. *aurea*
Euonymus radicans
,, *yedoensis*
Hydrangea petiolaris
Iris laevigata
Lilium auratum
"Golden-rayed Lily"
Lonicera japonica Halliana — also Korea and China
Magnolia kobus
,, *obovata*
,, *salicifolia*
,, *sieboldii* — also Korea
Malus sargentii
Primula japonica
Prunus serrulata
Rhododendron keiskii
R. schlippenbachii
R. yakusimanum

Sciadopitys verticillata
"Umbrella Pine"
Sorbus matsumurana
"Japanese Mountain Ash"
Sorbus rufo-ferruginea
Thalictrum kiusianum

Manipur

Rhododendron johnstoneanum
R. macabeanum also Assam

Korea

Abeliophyllum distichum
Syringa palibiniana

Nepal

Meconopsis dhwojii
" *napaulensis*
syn. *M. wallichii*
Polygonum affine
" " var. *Lowndes*
Primula prolifera

Persia

Gentiana septemfida
Prunus cerasifera var. *atropurpurea*
Tulipa clusiana also Iraq

Sikkim

Magnolia campbellii
Primula calderiana
" *mooreana*
" *sikkimensis* also Tibet

Tibet

Cyananthus sherriffae also Bhutan
Lilium wardii
Meconopsis betonicifolia

Meconopsis quintuplinervia	
,, *integrifolia*	also Burma and China
Primula alpicola var. *alba*	also Bhutan
,, ,, var. ,, *violacea*	
,, *florindae*	
Rhododendron leucaspis	
R. mollyanum	South-east
R. pemakoense	
R. tephropeplum	also Burma

U.S.S.R.

Brunnera macrophylla	Caucasus
Cephalaria tatarica	Siberia
Clematis alpina	North Russia
Eremurus robustus	Turkestan
Paeonia mlokosewitschii	Caucasus
Papaver commutatum	Caucasus
Puschkinia scilloides	Caucasus and Ararat
Rhododendron smirnowi	Caucasus
Tulipa eichleri	Trans Caucasus
,, *turkestanica*	Turkestan

CHAPTER XI

Wishes Fulfilled

After studying the list given in the previous chapter it is a matter of great interest to compare it with a list of the countries from which numbers of visitors come to see the garden; so here is a sample analysis of the overseas visitors who made their way to Inverewe in 1959:

United States, 214
Australia, 156
Canada, 130
South Africa, 81
New Zealand, 69
Nigeria, 57
France, 54
Germany, 47
Holland, 45
Sweden, 41
Denmark and India, each 32
Switzerland, 23
Belgium and Kenya, each 22
Eire, 20
Italy, 18
Southern Rhodesia, 17
West Indies, 12
Northern Rhodesia, 11
Ceylon, 9
Norway and the Sudan, each 8
Poland, Japan, Channel Islands, each 7
West Africa, 6
Pakistan and the Argentine, each 5
Malaya, 4

Thailand, Finland and Nyasaland, each 3
Arabia, Ghana, Somaliland, Persia, Israel, British Honduras, Uruguay, Venezuela, Spain, Luxemburg, Sierra Leone, Hong Kong, Cyprus, each 2
Borneo, Indonesia, Uganda, Madagascar, China, Persian Gulf, U.S.S.R., Greece, Portugal, Iraq, Chile, Hungary, Austria, each 1

The number of visitors has been growing steadily since then, but it is not easy to think of other countries from which they may have come, though no doubt the numbers from each increase as those people who have been go home and tell their friends about it. In fact many people informed us that they had been told of the garden and its attractiveness by friends who had already visited Britain and who had strongly advised them that, whatever else they should do in Britain, on no account should they fail to see Inverewe.

To illustrate this point one or two incidents are worth mentioning. An English visitor was on a holiday in New Zealand when a friend asked him if he had been to Inverewe and, when he admitted that he had not, his friend extracted a promise from him that he would do so on his return. He came, and told us the story of his introduction. A French family from Morocco signed the Overseas Visitors' book one day and it was noticed that they were carrying a well-worn copy of the brochure "Inverewe". When asked where they had procured it, they replied "from a son in Hong Kong". With his wife he had visited the garden earlier in the summer and, on returning to the Far East, he had stopped in Paris and told his family about his visit to Inverewe, gave them the booklet and recommended a visit. A visitor from Aberdeen, who had been round the garden, was waiting at the entrance for his sister who had lingered behind. She had arrived by air from Canada only two days before and when she apologised for keeping him waiting, she told him that the reason was that she had just been talking to a friend whom she had last met in Winnipeg three weeks earlier and neither of them had known that the other was going to Scotland.

An amusing custom we had started was to pin up a large map of the world in the reception office and ask overseas visitors to stick a pin in the spot from which they had come, and this showed people at a glance how widespread was the interest in the place.

It was Mrs. Sawyer's wish, when she handed over her garden to the National Trust for Scotland, that it should be enjoyed by many visitors from all over the world, but she was thinking in terms of hundreds rather than thousands and she spoke of 800 being a goodly number. Her very generous wish has been most abundantly fulfilled, but never in her wildest dreams did she think that just 10 years after her death over 60,000 visitors would wander happily in one year through this paradise that they had created. In fact she might have been staggered by the very thought, not quite realising how the opening up of the woodland by more and more paths could make it possible for such numbers of people to be dispersed unobtrusively through the policies.

Still less would she have dreamt of an "Inverewe Special" train being run from Edinburgh to Achnasheen, with buses to meet it and carry the passengers to Inverewe, and every seat on it booked in a very short time after it was advertised; or of large British India steamers carrying up to 800 visitors from Greenock to Inverewe. But all these things have happened and Inverewe has now become one of the major tourist attractions in the British Isles; an inspiration to garden lovers from all over the world.

This year (1964) over 400 of the world's leading botanists, including Russians and, it is hoped, Chinese as well, are expected to meet in Edinburgh for an international Botanical congress and, after about $8\frac{1}{2}$ days of lectures and discussions on botany, horticulture, forestry and agriculture, there will be a number of excursions to places of topical interest all over the British Isles. One of these excursions which bids fair to be about the most popular of all, will be a cruise on the steamer *Dunera* to Northern Ireland and the north-west of Scotland with Inverewe as one of its focal points.

Other cruises planned by the National Trust for Scotland will be making their way to Inverewe this year as before and so its popularity goes on growing and Osgood Mackenzie and Mairi Sawyer take their places amongst the great artists of the world—artists who have used Nature herself as their medium. Woodland forms an ideal setting for the gardener who wants to paint pictures in colour, but his work is beset by greater difficulties than that of the artist who paints with tubes of colour because his colours are provided by plants and he may have to wait for years to see them flower or, indeed he may never live to see this flowering; but he must have a picture in his mind's eye of what it will be like. Moreover, he has to remember that these colours will not all appear together, however much he allows for their usual times of flowering in the countries to which they have been introduced and he must create what will be a succession of pictures (better some years then others, of course) which will follow one after the other on the same spot. Parts of these pictures will be for ever changing, with the unpredictable weather producing sudden changes of light and cloud, bright sunlight and blue skies suddenly vanishing and a brilliantly coloured picture turning into a grey monochrome.

The artist who paints his pictures with a garden has the most exciting medium of all and the generations of people who follow do not have to debate as to whether they should clean the pictures or leave them with the dirt of ages dimming their colours. Nature renews her colours every year and, moreover, is constantly producing variation on her own original theme. In this way a great gardener can be one of the greatest of artists, but his medium has one great drawback and that is that his pictures will deteriorate if they are not cared for by artists who can understand them even if they could not have created them. Just as dirt collects on oil paintings, so the more rampant plants can quickly obscure the more beautiful ones which are less sturdy and the gardener must understand which plants need heavy pruning and which only need slight trimming into shape. Then the overhead canopy produced by the trees needs continual watching so that sufficient light is allowed to reach the undergrowth and it may be necessary to remove some of the trees that were planted close together in order to give enough shade when they were small.

A living picture like a garden needs careful handling all the time and it is this guardianship of Inverewe that the National Trust for Scotland have undertaken, a guardianship that carries with it a very heavy responsibility. They need the understanding help of all those who have seen and appreciated its beauty and the most obvious way in which they can give this help is by telling all their friends about what they have seen, in such glowing terms that they will not be content until they have seen it for themselves.

In this way the garden can become a rendezvous, as it often has already, for people to meet their friends—sometimes a party all coming together in a chartered 'bus for the summer outing of an organisation such as the Women's Guild of a Church, a Women's Rural Institute, a Farmers' Union or a school Nature Club; and often a quite unpremeditated meeting of friends who perhaps had not seen each other for years. We ourselves found that, during the summer months, scarcely a day passed without our meeting someone we had known somewhere, in England, Scotland or India, or on one of the Garden Cruises which my husband had organised for the National Trust for Scotland. Of course we had many visits at the house of friends and relations of Mrs. Sawyer and they will always be welcomed there.

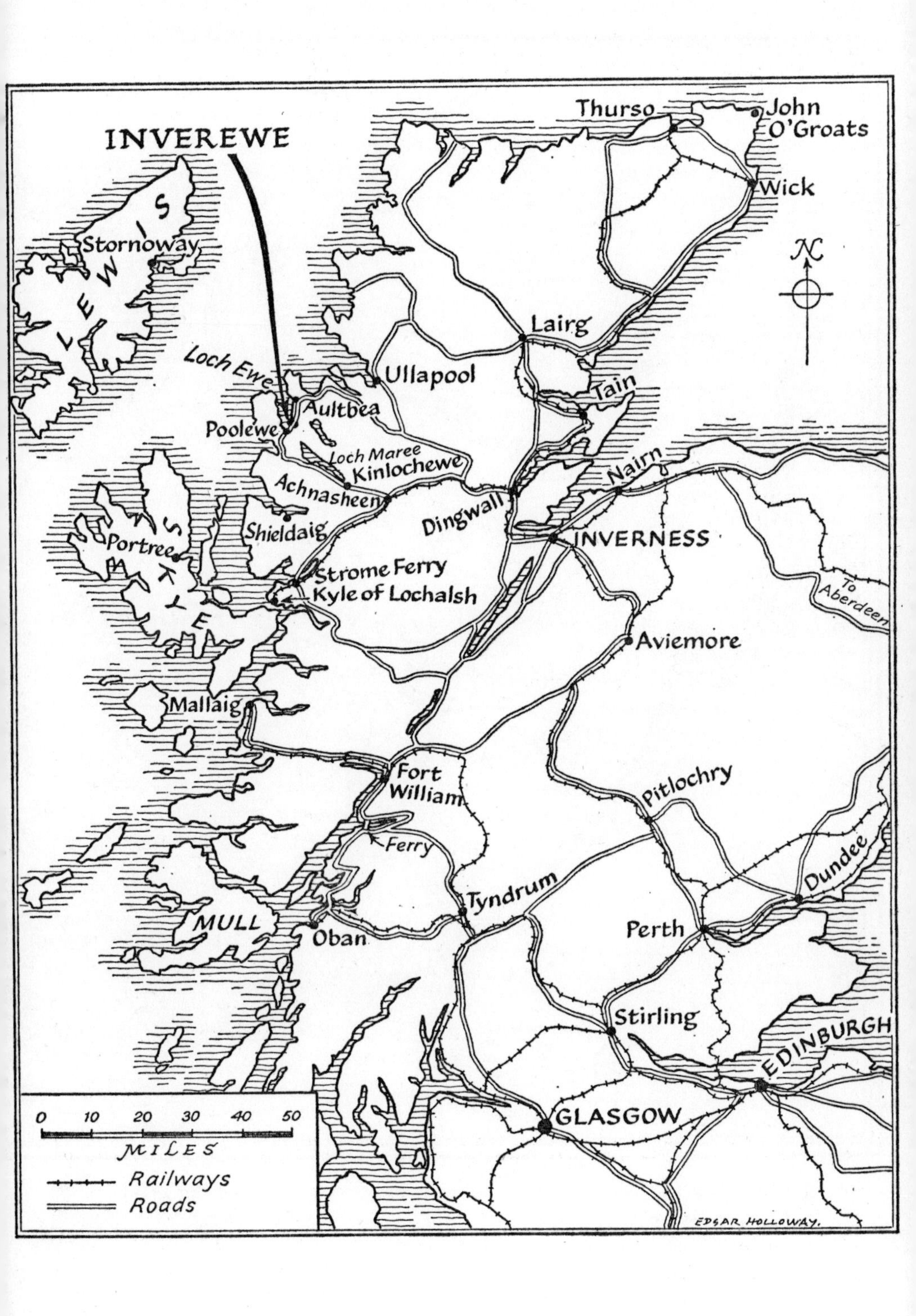
INVEREWE
Thurso
John O'Groats
Wick
LEWIS
Stornoway
Lairg
Loch Ewe
Ullapool
Tain
Aultbea
Poolewe
Loch Maree
Kinlochewe
Nairn
Achnasheen
Dingwall
Shieldaig
INVERNESS
Portree
SKYE
Strome Ferry
Kyle of Lochalsh
To Aberdeen
Aviemore
Mallaig
Fort William
Pitlochry
Ferry
Dundee
Tyndrum
MULL
Oban
Perth
Stirling
EDINBURGH
GLASGOW
0 10 20 30 40 50
MILES
Railways
Roads
EDGAR HOLLOWAY.

1. Gate Lodge
2. Summer House
3. Drive
4. Inverewe House
5. Rock Garden
6. "Japan"
7. Grove of Big Trees
8. Small Pond
9. Creag a Lios
10. Shelter Hut
11. Azaleas
12. View Point

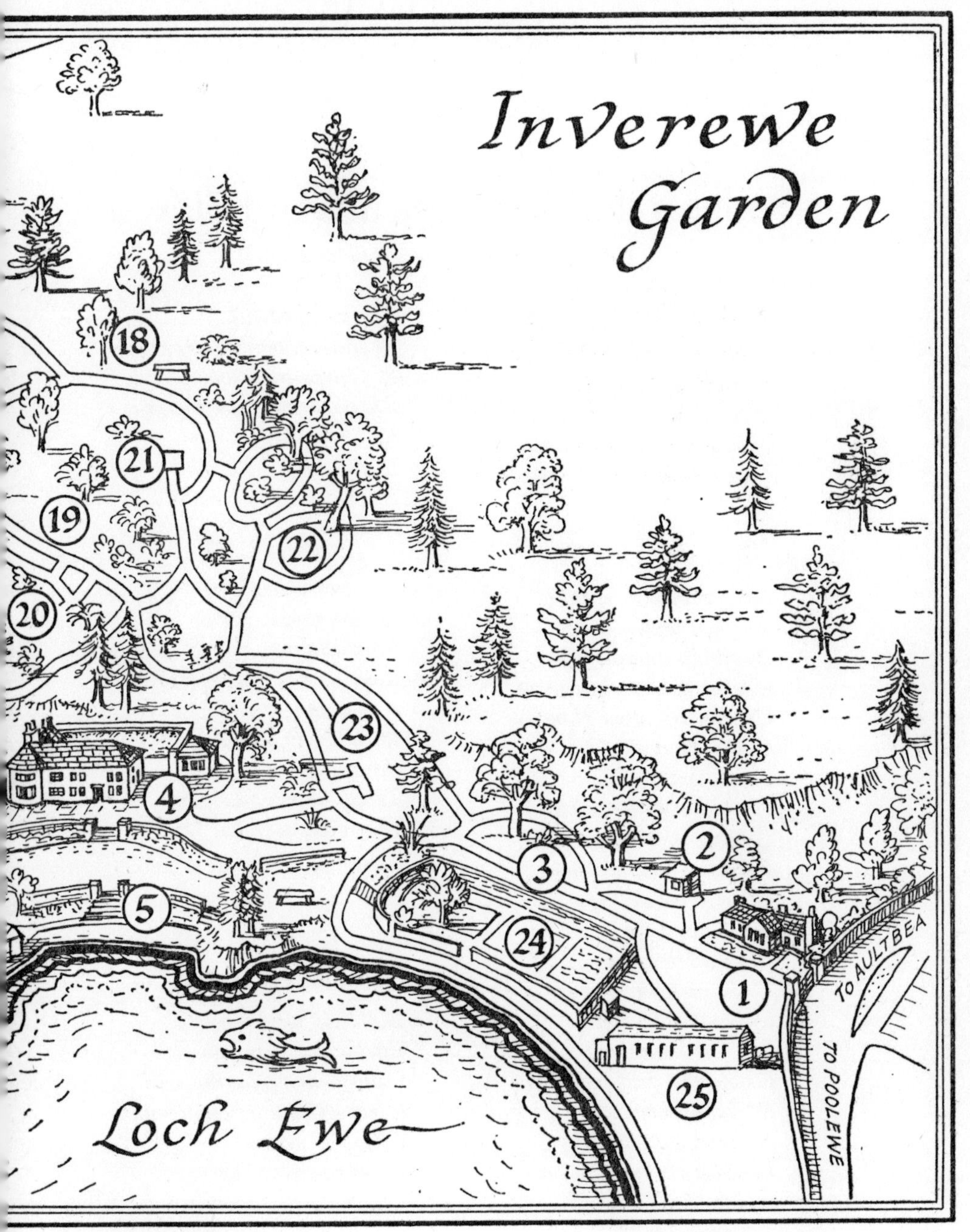

13. Shelter Hut
14. Large Pond
15. Cuddy Rock
16. The Bluff
17. Camas Glas
18. "Coronation Knoll"
19. Rhododendron Walk
20. R. sinogrande group
21. "Peace Plot"
22. "Bambooselem"
23. "America"
24. Walled Garden
25. Restaurant

K

Some of the Trees, Shrubs and Flowers

[*See the map on pages* 144 *and* 145]

1 and 2. Gate Lodge

Ceanothus × burkwoodii
Clianthus puniceus
Lavandula spica
Passiflora caerulea
Crinodendron hookerianum

3. Drive

Agapanthus orientalis
Arbutus unedo
Buddleia alternifolia
Cardiocrinum giganteum
Cedrus atlantica glauca
Cotoneaster frigida
C. × watereri
Cyclamen hederaefolia
Cytisus × praecox alba
Dierama pulcherrima
Erica arborea
E. carnea vars.
E. mediterranea
E. × veitchii
Eucryphia glutinosa
E. × nymansensis
Euphorbia griffithii
Fabiana imbricata
Hydrangea various
Libertia formosa
L. ixioides
Lilium hybrids
Magnolia sieboldii
Nerine bowdenii
Phormium tenax purpureum
P. taureo-striatum
Rhododendron arboreum
R. × "Elsae"
R. falconeri
R. fulgens
R. grande
R. griffithianum
R. oreotrephes
R. thomsonii
Rhus cotinus
Rosa farreri var. *persetosa*
R. moyesii
Rosmarinus officinalis
Senecio greyi
Tropaeolum speciosum
Watsonia beatricis
Yucca gloriosa

4. Inverewe House

Buddleia weyeriana
Carpodetus serratus
Ceanothus × burkwoodii
Ceratostigma willmottianum
Clematis alpina
C. montana rubens
Chaenomeles japonica
C. lagenaria cardinalis
Helleborus corsicus

Jasminum polyanthum
Lippia citriodora
Lonicera japonica halliana
Myrtus communis
Solanum crispum

5. Rock Garden

Anemone various
Campanula various
Caryopteris × clandonensis
C. tangutica
Celmisia hookeri
Cistus various
Codonopsis various
Cotoneaster frigida prostrata
Crinum powellii
Crocus spp.
Cyananthus integer
C. lobatus
C. sherriffiae
Delphinium nudicaule
D. tatsienense
Dianthus various
Dierama pulcherrima
Dodecatheon various
Erica various
Gazania various
Gentiana various
Geranium various
Hippeastrum pratensis
Helianthemum various
Iris innominata
I. reticulata
Jasione jankae
Leontopodium alpinum
Lewisia howellii
Linaria alpina
Meconopsis quintuplinervia
Melasphaerula graminea
Myosotidium hortensia
Narcissus dwarf spp.
Oxalis enneaphylla
Patrinia triloba
Penstemon various
Phlox various
Polygonum affine
P. vaccinifolium
Potentilla spp.
Primula various
Ramonda myconii
Raoulia australis
Rhodohypoxis baurri
Roscoea humeana
Salix boydii
Saxifraga various
Sedum various
Sempervivum various
Sisyrinchium various
Sternbergia lutea
Teucrium fruticans
Thalictrum kiousianum
T. reniforme
Tropaeolum polyphyllum
Tulipa spp.
Viola various

6. "Japan"

Arbutus menziesii
Beschorneria yuccoides
Camassia fraseri angusta
Cestrum newellii
Choisya ternata
Cordyline australis
Crinodendron hookerianum
Dicksonia antarctica
Dierama pulcherrima

Gladiolus "Ackerman"
Griselinia littoralis
Jovellana violacea
Libertia formosa
Lilium various
Meconopsis betonicifolia
M. grandis
M. napaulensis
Mitraria coccinea
Myosotidium hortensia
Paeonia delavayi
P. lutea
Philesia buxifolia
Polygonum vacciniifolium
Sorbus matsumurana
Trachycarpus fortunei
Tradescantia various

7. The Grove of Big Trees

Abies alba
Eucalyptus coccifera
Pseudotsuga douglasii
Sequoiadendron giganteum

8. Small Pond

Daboecea cantabrica
Escallonia "Pride of Donard"
Euonymus yedoensis
Iris chrysographes
I. laevigata
Malus sargentii
Meconopsis various
Primula various
Rhododendron augustinii
Rhododendron hybrids
Senecio clivorum "Othello"

9 and 10. Creag a Lios

Asteranthera ovata
Cytisus × beanii
C. × praecox
Celmisia hookeri
Erica various
Fothergilla major
Gentiana various
Hypericum olympicum
H. "Rowallane Hybrid"
Iris innominata
Primula various
Rhododendron davidsonianum
"Kurume Azaleas"
R. yakusimanum
Salix lapponum

11. Azaleas

Erica mediterranea
Nothofagus obliqua
N. procera
"Ghent hybrid" Azaleas
"Kurume Azaleas"
Rhododendron luteum
Sorbus vilmorinii
Taxodium distichum

12 and 13. View Point

Primula various
Rhododendron ambiguum
R. arboreum
R. barbatum
R. campanulatum
R. campylocarpum
R. ciliatum
R. davidsonianum
R. decorum

R. floccigerum
R. neriiflorum
R. niveum
R. rubiginosum
R. strigillosum
R. sutchuenense
R. yunnanense
Stranvaesia davidiana

14. The Large Pond

Arundinaria nitida
Arundo donax
Astilbe various
Cortaderia selloana
Desfontainea spinosa
Gunnera manicata
Hosta various
Hydrangea paniculata
Iris laevigata
Nymphaea various
Olearia macrodonta
O. semidentata
Osmunda regalis
Pernettya mucronata
Primula florindae
Rodgersia aesculifolia
Rosa moyesii
Rubus tricolor
Scilla peruviana
Typha angustifolia
T. latifolia

15. Cuddy Rock

Camellia hybrids
Eucryphia × nymanensis
Magnolia salicifolia
Malus × eleyi
Olearia semidentata
Sorbus vilmorinii

16. The Bluff

Dwarf Heaths
Dwarf Rhododendrons
Schizophragma hydrangeoides

17. Camas Glas

Drimys aromatica
D. winteri
Gevuina avellana
Rhododendron arboreum
R. arizelum
R. auriculatum
R. barbatum
R. brachysiphon
R. campylocarpum
R. crassum
R. dalhousiae
R. decorum
R. desquamatum
R. elliottii
R. falconeri
R. giganteum
R. griersonianum
R. hodgsonii
R. insigne
R. johnstoneanum
R. lindleyi
R. macabeanum
R. maddenii
R. magnificum
R. manipurense
R. mollyanum
R. rubiginosum
R. sinogrande
R. smirnowi
R. stewartianum
R. sutchuenense
R. taggianum

R. thomsonii
R. triflorum
R. wightii
R. yunnanense

18. "Coronation Knoll"

Cornus florida rubra
Embrothrium lanceolatum
Eucalyptus spp.
Podocarpus spicata
Rhododendrons "Inverewe hybrids"

19. Rhododendron Walk

Crinodendron hookerianum
Drimys winteri
Olearia macrodonta
Peltiphyllum peltatum syn. *Saxifraga peltata*
Populus lasiocarpa
Rhododendron diaprepes gargantua
R. fictolacteum
R. giganteum
R. macabeanum
R. micranthum
R. neriiflorum
R. oreodoxa
R. sinogrande
R. wardii

20. R. sinogrande group

Meconopsis various
Primula various
Rhododendron hodgsonii
R. macabeanum
R. meddianum
R. "Roylmadd"
R. sinogrande
R. "Sir Charles Lemon"
R. souliei
R. thomsonii
R. wightii
Salix magnifica
Trillium spp.

21. "Peace Plot"

Gaultheria various
Halesia monticola versicolor
Ramonda myconii
Ranunculus lyallii
Rhododendron barbatum
R. campanulatum
R. campylocarpum
R. "Cornubia"
R. "Countess of Haddington"
R. dalhousiae
R. decorum
R. × *emasculum*
R. eximium
R. "Fabia"
R. falconeri
R. "Fragrantissimum"
R. gibsonii
R. giganteum
R. glaucophyllum
R. "Glory of Penjerrick"
R. griersonianum
R. johnstoneanum
R. lacteum
R. leucaspis
R. lindleyi
R. "Loder's White"
R. megeratum

R. neriiflorum
R. niveum
R. orbiculare
R. "Princess of Orange"
R. rhabdotum
R. smirnowi
R. thomsonii
R. wightii
R. williamsianum
R. yunnanense
R. zeylanicum

22. "Bambooselem"

Abutilon vitifolium
Aristotelia racemosa
Arundinaria nitida
Azara petiolaris
Bambusa aurea
B. nigra
B. palmata
Beschorneria yuccoides
Billardiera longiflora
Buddleia auriculata
B. colvilei
B. hybrids various
Camellia various
Clematis armandii
Clethra alnifolia
C. arborea
Cornus kousa
Daphne blagayana
Davidia involucrata
Drimys aromatica
Eccremocarpus scaber
Embrothrium coccineum
E. longifolium
Erythronium americanum
Eucalyptus coccifera
E. cordata
E. gunnii
E. pauciflora
E. salicifolia
Eucryphia glutinosa
E. moorei
Genista aetnensis
Gentiana asclepiadea
G. sino-ornata
Gevuina avellana
Gordonia altamaha
Hoheria lyallii
Hydrangea petiolaris
Leptospermum nichollsii
Lilium auratum
Lonicera × heckrottii
L. tragophylla
Magnolia campbellii
M. delavayi
M. × lennei
M. salicifolia
M. stellata
Myrtus luma
Narcissus cyclamineus
N. nanus
Osmanthus delavayi
Pieris formosa
Pittosporum eugenioides
P. ralphii
P. tenuifolium
Podocarpus totara
Primula helodoxa
P. "Inverewe"
Senecio rotundifolius
Stewartia serrata
Trillium grandiflorum

23. "America"

Azalea various
Berberidopsis corallina
Buddleia colvilei
Cardiocrinum giganteum
Cypripedium calceolus
Dianella tasmanica
Eucalyptus coccifera
Garrya elliptica
Hydrangea sargentiana
Iris various
Lilium de Graaf hybrids
Magnolia kobus
Rhododendron Nobleanum
Syringa various
Veronica various
Viburnum × *bodnantense*

24. Walled Garden

Acanthus latifolius
Callistermon citrinus
Ceanothus various
Cestrum purpureum
Clematis indivisa lobata
Cordyline australis
Gladiolus "Ackerman"
Mutisia oligodon
Myosotidium hortensia
Schizostylis coccinea

25. Restaurant

Cytisus battandieri
Libertia formosa
Phormium tenax